Effectively Staffing Your Law Firm

jennifer j. rose, editor

GP|Solo
ABA General Practice, Solo & Small Firm Division

ABA
Defending Liberty
Pursuing Justice

Cover design by ABA Publishing

13 12 11 10 09 5 4 3 2 1

Cataloging-in-Publication data is on file with the Library of Congress

Staff in the law office / Rose, Jennifer J., ed.

Discounts are available for books ordered in bulk. Special consideration is given to state bars, CLE programs, and other bar-related organizations. Inquire at Book Publishing, ABA Publishing, American Bar Association, 321 North Clark Street, Chicago, Illinois 60654.

www.ababooks.org

Contents

About the Editor

Jennifer J. Rose was a solo practitioner practicing family law in rural Shenandoah, Iowa, for more than 20 years before moving to Morelia, Michoacán, Mexico, 11 years ago. In that life, she was listed in *Best Lawyers in America*, rated AV by Martindale-Hubbell, and served a stint as chair of the Iowa State Bar Association Family and Juvenile Law Section.

Jennifer served as editor-in-chief of *GP|Solo*, the flagship magazine of the American Bar Association General Practice, Solo and Small Firm Division, from 1995 to 2007; served on the Division's Council; and served on too many committees and boards to enumerate. She is vice chair of the ABA General Practice, Solo and Small Firm Division, destined to become chair in the 2010–2011 bar year.

She has also served terms on the ABA Standing Committee on Continuing Education of the Bar and the Standing Committee on Publishing Oversight. She has served as list manager and "den mother" for the listserv Solosez, sponsored by the ABA General Practice, Solo and Small Firm Division.

Jennifer has been a contributing editor to *Matrimonial Strategist* and *Internet Law Researcher*, in addition to having served as a judge of *Law Office Computing*'s annual law firm Web site competition. She also was editor of the *How to Capture and Keep Clients* (American Bar Association, 2005).

She publishes (and neglects) a blog at http://www.stufflawyerslike.wordpress.com and at http://staringatstrangers.com.

About the Contributors

David J. Abeshouse practices business litigation and alternative dispute resolution law in Uniondale, Long Island, New York. He has maintained his law office in an executive suite just a few miles from home for more than seven years. He also is a professional neutral, serving as an arbitrator on the commercial arbitration panels of two national ADR forums. His Web site is www.BizLawNY.com, and he can be reached at David@BizLawNY.com.

Jeffrey Allen is solo practitioner in the firm of Graves & Allen (http://www.gravesallen.com/) in Oakland, California, with a practice emphasis in real estate, bankruptcy, and litigation. He is editor-in-chief and columnist for the "Technology Practice Guide" issues of the magazine *GP|Solo*, published by the American Bar Association General Practice, Solo and Small Firm Division, and he serves on the *ABA Journal* Board of Editors. His e-mail address is jallenlaw@aol.com.

Jennifer J. Ator of Miami-area law firm Hankins & Ator (http://www.hankinsator.com/) represents both plaintiffs and defendants in commercial and employment litigation matters in state and federal courts. She has written and published extensively on employment law topics and is a Florida Supreme Court Certified Circuit Court mediator. She has served in the American Bar Association House of Delegates and the Florida Bar Young Lawyers Division Board of Governors, and is active in the ABA General Practice, Solo and Small Firm Division, where she sits on its council and edits the "Best of Sections" issues of the *GP|Solo* magazine.

Jim Calloway is director of the Oklahoma Bar Association's Management Assistance Program, past co-chair of the ABA TechShow and the National Solo and Small Firm Conferences, and a prolific writer and speaker on legal technology issues, Internet research, law-office management and organization, and legal ethics. The publisher of Jim Calloway's Law Practice Tips Blog (http://jimcalloway.typepad.com/), he can be reached at jimc@okbar.org.

Therese A. Cannon currently serves as associate director of the Senior Commission of the Western Association of Schools and Colleges and has served as dean of two law schools, most recently John F. Kennedy University School of Law, and as dean or director of two paralegal programs. She was the educational consultant to the American Bar Association Standing Committee on Paralegals for 10 years and previously served on both the committee and its Approval Commission, including three years as chair. She is the author of *Ethics and Professional Responsibility for Legal Assistants, 3d ed.*, and *A Concise Guide to Paralegal Ethics,* published by Aspen Law & Business, as well as two reference manuals for the ABA Standing Committee on Paralegals for program directors seeking approval, and co-authored *Paralegals, Profitability, and the Future of Your Law Practice* with Arthur G. Greene for the ABA Law Practice Management Section.

Laura V. Farber, a partner with Hahn & Hahn LLP (http://www.hahnlawyers.com/), practices litigation with an emphasis on employment disputes, wrongful termination lawsuits, and wage and hour disputes. She has served on the ABA Commission on Domestic Violence, Commission on Youth at Risk, Tort Trial and Insurance Section Law in the Public Service Committee, House of Delegates Nominating and Select Committees, and *ABA Journal* Board of Editors, and is past chair of the Young Lawyers Division. She is secretary of the ABA General Practice, Solo and Small Firm Division. A member of the Latina Lawyers Bar Association and the Hispanic National Bar Association, Farber has been named one of the top 50 women lawyers in Los Angeles. She has been featured in the *Los Angeles Business Journal* and received the 2003 American Bar Association's Commission on Ethnic and Racial Diversity in the Profession–Spirit of Excellence Award and the 2004 YWCA San Gabriel Valley Women of Excellence in the Law Award.

Susan D. Goldstein is a recruiter with Dougherty & Associates (http://lawsearch-sf.com/) in San Francisco. She has been a law office administrator and support staff recruiter and was operations manager at the attorney search firm of Major, Hagen & Africa.

Nancy Byerly Jones is an attorney, certified mediator, legal management advisor, and author of *Easy Self-Audits for the Busy Law Office* (ABA 1999). She previously practiced law and served as management counsel for the North Carolina State Bar. Her consulting work and seminars focus primarily on law firms and corporate legal departments. Nancy's company's Web site is www.nbjconsulting.com, and she can be reached at nbj@nbjconsulting.com.

Jim Karger and his unique approach to employee relations have been the subject of articles in the *Wall Street Journal*, *BusinessWeek*, *Texas Business*, and many other publications. After 30 years as a valued advisor to hundreds of companies and industry associations, he has developed a systematic approach to improve communications, relationships, and connections in the workplace. He is a popular speaker on workplace topics. A recovering labor relations lawyer in Dallas, he is co-founder of the San Miguel Leadership Institute, in San Miguel de Allende, Mexico. His Web site is www.crediblyconnect.com.

David Zachary Kaufman grew up in Mexico and came to the United States to live in 1968. The Fairfax, Virginia, solo practitioner focuses his practice upon appeals, corporate and business matters, litigation, unfair business practices, and real estate and dirt law, lecturing lawyers and other professionals on personal and business security issues and answering their questions in his spare time. He sits on the editorial board of "Best of Sections" issues of *GP|Solo* magazine, published by the ABA General Practice, Solo and Small Firm Division. His law firm Web site is http://www.BusinessBrawls.com, and his blog can be found at http://www.QuiCustodes.typepad.com.

Robert A. Kraft is a principal in Kraft & Associates (http://www.kraftlaw.com/), a Dallas personal injury firm. He is currently a director emeritus of the Dallas Trial Lawyers Association and is president of the North Dallas Bar Association. Kraft is a fellow of the College of the State Bar of Texas and a sustaining member of the National Organization of Social Security Claimants Representatives and the Texas Trial Lawyers Association.

David Leffler is a member of the New York City law firm Leffler Marcus & McCaffrey LLC (http://www.lmmlawfirm.com/), where he represents technology clients, women-owned businesses, and other entrepreneurial and growing companies. The law firm also represents clients in commercial litigation. Leffler has been engaged in a wide variety of transactions and matters in the areas of corporate, business, real estate, employment, Internet/new media, and intellectual property law. He writes a column, "Being Solo," which appears in *GP|Solo* magazine, published by the ABA General Practice, Solo and Small Firm Division. His e-mail address is lefflermailbox@aol.com.

Jean Maneke, of The Maneke Law Group, L.C. (http://www.manekelaw.com/), Kansas City, Missouri, practices primarily in the areas of media, entertainment, and probate law, serving as counsel to the Missouri Press Association. She represents authors, publishers, film producers, photographers, musicians, and others in creative arts fields. She sits on the board of the Missouri Broadcasters Association and the Missouri Press-Bar Commission, and she is chair of the Missouri Bar Media Law Committee.

Hope Viner Samborn is a lawyer and freelance writer in Chicago. She is co-author of *The Legal Research and Writing Handbook: A Basic Approach for Paralegals* (Aspen Publishers, 2008).

Lyza L. Sandgren is a paralegal and president of CanopyLegal, LLC (http://canopylegal.com/), based in Buford, Georgia, providing intellectual property software sales and training services to legal professionals, law firms, and corporate legal departments as well as offering contract trademark and copyright paralegal and docketing services to small firms and solo practitioners.

Sheryl Sisk Schelin is a solo practitioner in North Myrtle Beach, South Carolina, where she focuses upon consumer bankruptcy, consumer litigation, and plaintiff's employment law. She publishes The South Carolina Employment Law Blog (http://scemploymentlaw.com/), The South Carolina Bankruptcy & Consumer Law Blog (http:// scbankruptcyblog.com/), and The Inspired Solo (http://inspiredsolo. wordpress.com/. She can be reached at s.schelin@gmail.com.

Lisa Solomon was one of the first lawyers to recognize and take advantage of the technological advances that make outsourcing legal research and writing services practical and profitable for law firms of all sizes. Since 1996, Solomon has limited her Ardsley, New York, practice to assisting lawyers across the country with all of their legal research and writing needs, including preparing and arguing appeals and drafting substantive motions and trial memoranda. She has worked in almost every area of law, and has developed particular expertise in insurance coverage, negligence, family law, trusts and estates, and contract matters. Her Web site is http://www.QuestionOfLaw.net.

Robert C. ("T.J.") Thurston is a solo practicing at Thurston Law Offices (http://www.thurstonlawpc.com) in Huntley, Illinois, where he is also the chief cook, typist, and bottlewasher. He concentrates his practice on assisting individuals and small business in managing their legal affairs. He also has had significant experience in Internet legal technologies and legal issues surrounding the Internet. He publishes the Thurston Law Office Blog at http://thurstonlawpc.wordpress.com/.

Ted A. Waggoner practices in a small firm, Peterson & Waggoner, LLP (http://www.peterson-waggoner.com/), in Rochester, Indiana. A general practitioner with an emphasis on real estate, estate planning, and business issues, Ted has focused on business-planning concerns for a variety of clients and is a civil mediator. He is active with the Indiana State Bar Association and the Indiana Bar Foundation, where he serves as chair of the Fellows. Ted is a Fellow of the American Bar Foundation.

Robin Page West practices with the small firm Cohan & West (http://www.cohanwest.com) in Baltimore, Maryland, where she specializes in qui tam and whistleblower litigation, negligence, and products liability. She was editor-in-chief of the American Bar Association General Practice, Solo and Small Firm Division *SOLO* newsletter from its inception until 2006, serves on the ABA General Practice Solo and Small Firm Division Council, and is a member of its Publications Board. She is the author of *Advising the Qui Tam Whistleblower: From Identifying a Case to Filing under the False Claims Act, Second Edition.*

William I. Weston is dean of the School of Legal Studies, Kaplan University, in Florida. He was previously an associate dean and professor of law at Concord Law School and a member of the faculty at Kaplan University. He has more than 30 years of teaching experience and has been widely published. He is active in the American Bar Association, where he chairs the Standing Committee on Professional Responsibility of the General Practice, Solo and Small Firm Division and the Committee on Ethics and Technology of the Center for Professional Responsibility. He can be reached at bweston@kaplan.edu.

About This Book

In only 10 television seasons, Murphy Brown went through some 93 secretaries. *L.A. Law*'s McKenzie, Brackman, Chaney & Kuzak had Benny Stulwitz, the mentally challenged office worker. Real-life California lawyer Edward L. Masry had Erin Brockovich. And, of course, Perry Mason had Della Street. So, who's helping you get the work done?

Every lawyer in a solo or small firm likes to think that only those who've taken the oath and been admitted to the bar are at the helm, but the reality is that the engine driving the office is the staff. The first point of contact many clients have with a lawyer can be the voice on the telephone or the receptionist—the face of the law office. The back-office toilers are the ones who make it all happen. And then there are the invisible souls—the outsourced ghost-writer and researcher, the hired-for-the-job transcriptionist, and the virtual staff. In many firms, one employee may wear several hats at the same time.

Lawyers are practicing with more staff than ever—and with less. Say goodbye to the days when a solo or small firm's staff amounted to a secretary. Della Street's role as Gal Friday has met up with specialists in finance, marketing, human resources, information technology, word processing, library services, records management, office management, mailroom, and practice support. Legal assistants now perform many tasks that once were solely within a lawyer's domain. Say hello, at the other extreme, to a new era of prosperous and respected lawyers who do it all by themselves without a single employee.

We've gone from the times when it was just assumed that the supporting roles in law office staff were held by women to wondering whether secretaries should be asked to make coffee, tidy up the office, and pick up the dry cleaning. There was a time when only a rare lawyer would publicly admit to typing: women lawyers who typed risked being mistaken for secretaries, and male lawyers risked their manhood.

The quaint art of typing slowly grew into word processing. Before long, the siren call of computers lured many a lawyer into keyboarding. Then, lawyers who used to dictate to legal secretaries trained in ancient and secret languages like Gregg shorthand moved up to Dictaphones, which were supplanted by voice-recognition technologies that rendered contacts between lawyer and staff superfluous. Refined programs for document and case management, coupled with lawyers' growing skills at using them, put the role of support staff in further jeopardy—as did a new player in the law office: the paralegal or legal assistant. The crossover is ironic: Lawyers adopted the roles previously relegated to support staff, while paralegals and legal assistants took over many of the labor-intensive chores in the lawyer's domain.

Good law office staff is harder to find (and keep) than clients and, sometimes, spouses. Not a mere receptionist/typist/filing clerk, a good support staff can be the lawyer's alter ego, right arm, custodian, den mother, rabbi, and guardian angel. Could you manage if your staff didn't show up tomorrow morning?

The lawyers and law office staff who contributed to this book come from a broad range of practice settings and styles. Some are nearly old enough to be recently retired from the active practice of law, some teach and consult, and some are still toiling in the fields of the law. Each has had hands-on, practical experience owning and operating a solo or small law firm, and each has shared his or her expertise generously in the development of this book.

Part I
Going It Alone

There is a growing trend among lawyers to do entirely without human hired help. No longer characterized as eccentric loners, these lawyers practice with the 24/7 assistance of electronic staff. Technology has made "lawyers who type" socially acceptable and Blackberries, e-mail, and cell phones have created a cadre of lawyers who practice as efficiently as many who boast fully staffed offices. The do-it-yourself trend has caught on like wildfire. Can you do it all yourself—or do you need help?

To Staff, or Not to Staff: That Is the Question

1

by Hope Viner Samborn

Do you have to use your arms like windshield wipers just to get through the mounds of paper you encounter daily as you walk into your office? Do you fantasize about streamlining your work with technology? Do you wonder whether hiring a paralegal or purchasing new technology could help you handle your paperwork woes, draft forms, research legal issues, or interview clients? The following quiz can help you determine whether you are better off with hardware and software or with a living, breathing legal assistant.

1. **How do you refer to your computer?**
   a. By a nickname like HAL, maybe followed by its RAM size, like HAL256.
   b. "That *&%$#ing machine!"
   c. The dust collector in the corner.
   d. What computer?

2. **What do you carry in your pockets?**
   a. A handheld PDA, a pager, an HP Capshare, and a cell phone.

b. A lot of lint, paper clips, rubberbands, and a Bates stamper.
c. A fistful of Post-it notes reminding you of tasks to do and people to call.
d. Your hands, with change to use to call your mother to tell her you won't be practicing law anymore.

3. How organized is your office?

a. You have taken the paperless office route. You scan every document or form, making each accessible via your computer.
b. Wires abound. You have power cords and surge protectors plugged into every outlet, but three inches of dust coat each machine.
c. Every inch of your desk is covered with crisscrossed stacks of paper, some obscuring your view.
d. You don't know because you haven't been in there in months.

4. How do you feel about the extra paperwork involved in payroll?

a. You have a wonderful secretary who can handle everything you throw at her, including keeping track of payroll; or you have the software and hardware to handle the job, and you know how to use it.
b. You are anxious to take on more paperwork. Bookkeeping, payroll taxes, and benefit itemization are welcome distractions from legal work.
c. Keeping track of payroll, taxes, and benefits makes you feel like the dentist is extracting your front teeth every two weeks.
d. You have a hard time keeping track of your own salary.

5. How are your balance sheets?

a. You are raking in the money and don't know how to spend it fast enough.
b. Small expenditures every two to four months for software are the norm.
c. Large outlays of cash and long-term financial commitments, such as 30-year mortgages, give you hives.
d. The thought of doing math makes you want to hibernate.

6. Is your cash flow steady?

a. Everything in your office is consistent. You earn the same amount of money every month and know exactly where it comes from.

b. Your earnings vary; however, they never go below a certain amount of money.

c. Some months, the cash trickles in and the rent is overdue.

d. You have yet to be in the black.

7. How much space does your practice occupy?

a. You have a spacious office, but every corner is filled with computers, printers, fax machines, copy machines, telephones, and shredders.

b. You work out of a 10-by-10 home office just a few feet away from the breakfast table and have additional space in the basement.

c. You have an extra office that provides climate-controlled storage for boxes of paperwork you should have sorted and filed six months ago.

d. Not much. I don't need that much space, because I don't spend that much time working.

8. What type of office equipment do you have?

a. You have two networked workstation computers, a server, a laptop, scanner, printer, copier/fax, headset phone system, and a captain's chair that allows you to swivel among them.

b. You have a PC, printer, scanner, and fax stationed at a U-shaped desk for optimum efficiency, and a three-line phone plugged into a digital answering machine.

c. You have a standard rectangle desk, with the processor under the desk at your feet and the monitor keyboard and mouse taking up the desktop. You put the keyboard on top of the monitor when you want to jot down some notes or review files.

d. You have a nerfball hoop in the corner and can shoot the lights out.

9. How well do you keep up with the changes in technology?

a. You read every computer magazine on the market, monitor several technology discussion groups including ABA-

LAWTECH, and hire a consultant regularly to reassess your technology needs.

b. You make small software changes when you can afford them, but regularly update your virus protection. If a colleague mentions a new product that sounds intriguing, you investigate it and may buy it if you have the cash flow.
c. You use Windows 3.11, having upgraded from DOS just a few years ago. You figure it still works, why replace it?
d. Those fountain pens with replaceable cartridges sure are swell.

10. How large is your list of clients and potential clients?

a. You know everyone in town, send an e-mail newsletter to everyone you meet, and have an active website that explains your services and provides substantive information for viewers. You coach three sports teams, are active in the community, and regularly conduct seminars to attract new clients.
b. You are very busy with the clients you have and are always trying to find new ways of meeting additional clients.
c. You have one good corporate client; the rest are family and close friends.
d. You spend each morning scanning the obituaries.

11. How often do you go out to lunch?

a. You regularly go out to lunch with colleagues, friends, and clients. If you don't see people, you are bored and lonely.
b. You occasionally go out to lunch, but you usually work out instead with a friend, colleague, or client. It's the only time you can manage to get in that exercise.
c. You rarely venture out of the office and instead pack your lunch so you can continue working. Besides, you don't want to see anyone who might ask you a lot of personal questions.
d. You rarely eat lunch, preferring to send out for another triple-shot espresso instead.

12. Are you able to train staff?

a. You are a patient teacher and work with someone until he or she understands what you want them to do, even if it takes a while.

b. You are willing to teach new skills, but your time is limited, and you prefer people who are quick studies and who are easily adaptable.
c. Anyone you hire has to know how to use your software. Who has time to teach?
d. First you have to learn what to do.

13. How do you usually communicate with clients?

a. You e-mail them regularly and automatically send status reports on a weekly basis. Client files are always a mouse click away, or, in your PDA if you're meeting out of the office.
b. You try to provide regular updates, but things get in the way. You occasionally send a letter or call with a brief update; if they call you, you dictate a memo to file.
c. You update clients only on an "as-needed" basis. What they don't know won't hurt them.
d. You use form letters.

14. Why did you go into a solo practice?

a. You wanted to control your work, your finances, and your environment. You also wanted more time with your family.
b. You want to build your career and like to work hard, even if you have no outside life other than the SOLOSEZ discussion group.
c. You're still working on your resume.
d. You don't want to join a firm that would hire someone like you.

Answers

If you answered "a" for most, if not all, of the questions, you are a technology wizard with a thriving legal practice. A paralegal could enhance your output, but only if the workload is more than you can handle.

If you answered "b" for most questions, a legal assistant could help even though your finances appear to be sound. You have a stable cash flow, although it ebbs and flows. You probably have adequate space to house a staff member but could use someone to help you get rid of the clutter in both your office and your mind. You have no time to keep abreast of technological changes or advances, and an employee could help a lot in this area. You are open to new networking opportunities.

If you answered "c" for most questions, you need help. A paralegal could help manage the mountains of paper, promote efficiency, and better utilize your resources. Unfortunately, you are not ready to hire one. You don't have the stable cash flow to handle an employee and your time is as limited as your patience. Training someone would be a challenge that would likely be insurmountable. Expecting someone to be able to walk in and grasp your organizational "system" is unrealistic. You may be more suited for a hermit-type existence where contact with other human beings is limited to clients, e-mail, instant messages, and the telephone. But if you get organized and become stable, you may want to think about hiring a legal assistant to enhance your practice.

If you answered "d" to most, if not all, questions, think about making that call to your mom.

2

When You're the Lawyer, Secretary, Receptionist, and Janitor: Doing It All Without Staff

by Robert C. ("T.J.") Thurston

Have you ever been confused about how you should dress for work? I'm not talking about the debate between a suit and jeans. I mean which hat do you wear that day? The receptionist hat? The secretary hat? The law clerk hat? The IT guy hat? The janitor hat? The bookkeeping hat? The lawyer hat? Or do you put all of them on at once? And how do you balance all those hats on your head without diving into the bottle of Tylenol?

This is the dilemma faced by all solo attorneys and even many smaller law offices that don't have separate people for all those jobs. The question is essentially how to handle all these tasks and assure a smoothly running law practice. The answer lies somewhere in the spectrum between efficient time and resource management and hiring help.

Most lawyers handle very similar daily tasks, whether you are a solo or work in a very large office. These tasks are, not in order of significance, answering client calls; doing legal research; preparing forms or documents; communicating with opposing counsel and/or vendors; coordinating schedules; docketing deadlines; billing and administrative tasks (yes, even filing deserves your attention once in a while); court appearances; and the necessary water cooler break. As most attorneys know, these tasks can take up about 100 hours of a 40-hour work week; if you're a solo, perhaps more.

What to do, what to do?

Managing Time and Resources

In this technological age, the first logical resource is . . . well, technology. Use of technology should be focused on increasing efficiency. If it will take you two weeks to learn how to use the new gadget, it is not a wise use of your time. In addition, if it is outdated technology or adds too much incremental cost, it is not a wise choice of equipment.

For example, there is little or no reason to have a stand-alone single-function fax machine any more. Very few practice areas are still using this antiquated machine. For those who still have the need or use of faxes, a smarter choice is a service like eFax (http://www.efax.com) or Fax2Mail (http://www.fax2mail.com), where you can send faxes direct from your computer and receive faxes in your e-mail inbox. You achieve the same task, but your additional incremental cost is very low because you are using your existing computer, Internet, and e-mail technologies.

Another useless waste of time is making trips to the post office. This is not billable and typically takes much longer than you plan. Most solos and small firms don't have their own shipping department. Instead, you can either buy stamps by mail from the Postal Service (http://www.usps.com) or use a service like Stamps.com (http://www.stamps.com) to handle all your postage needs in your small office, while tracking the costs to bill them back to your client. This is a highly efficient way to get mail out the door.

You need to rely heavily on the Internet. Not only does this make you more efficient, but it will also save you a lot of money. Why pay for bound volumes of the court rules when they are all available online? If your state bar association pays for use of a free legal research service such as FastCase (http://www.fastcase.com), why pay for Westlaw or LexisNexis? In addition, a lot of court and other resources are available online, such as court forms, law review articles, and e-mail lists, such as Solosez (http://www.solosez.net), that can answer a lot of your questions.

There are some "low-tech" solutions to the time management dilemma as well. Here are a few tips:

Don't take every phone call (also known as "that's what voicemail is for"). If you are in the middle of a task, interrupting that task to answer the phone creates massive inefficiency in the original task. Let's use drafting a brief as an example. You are in the middle of a key issue and trying to reconcile case law with your argument. The phone rings. If you answer the call, it will likely cause two problems: (1) you forget the great point you were just about to incorporate into the brief and (2) the phone call creates a new emergency task for a different client. One caveat to this tip: answering client calls by the attorney tends to win clients' favor because they are used to "gatekeepers" (such as secretaries or voicemail) preventing them from reaching the attorneys.

Prioritize assignments based on legal deadlines. This seems obvious (from a malpractice standpoint), but does carry a downside from a client-satisfaction perspective. The client who wants a will drafted next week may be a lower priority than an emergency motion for a protective order. This is often a difficult choice to make and many clients don't understand why their project is not the highest priority. There is also the "hidden" and dangerous priority of finance. You may be tempted to perform work for clients who are paying at a higher rate or on a more regular basis. This is a personal decision, but always remember that a dissatisfied client is likely to have greater impact on your practice than the hourly rate for a happy client.

Schedule time for administrative needs. Disorganization breeds inefficiency. If you don't know where something is, the time you take to find it when you really need it is wasted time. File organization, ordering supplies, and even marketing require a portion of your time and if you don't schedule those tasks, they won't get done. Although the funny video with the monkey somebody e-mailed to you is more entertaining than filing, step away from the computer for a short bit, and do yourself a favor by paying attention to these sleeping monsters we call "nonbillable work."

When to Get Help

Even though as a solo or small firm lawyer you admittedly have the powers of a superhero, even superheroes need sidekicks sometimes. You need to recognize when and how to get help. This is not a rallying cry to ramp up your staff to four secretaries, three bookkeepers, two law clerks, and a partridge in a pear tree. Rather, many tasks can be subcontracted to an outside service or handled by a part time employee.

The key to knowing when it is time to set the ego aside and allow someone into your cloister is when the nonbillable tasks are taking up more of your time than the billable tasks. If you find that you are doing more paralegal or clerical work on your files and you don't have time to draft the motions or documents your clients have requested, you need help. If you find you are answering too many unsolicited phone calls from people who want free legal advice and it is distracting you from your work, you need help.

Again, technology comes to the rescue. There are such animals as "virtual offices." These creatures would not have boarded Noah's Ark two by two, but they sure come in handy when you want a professional face to the outside world while you are away from the office or phone. For example, a service like OneBox (http://www.onebox.com) will answer your phones, take messages, forward calls, handle faxes, set up conferences, coordinate schedules, and handle many other daily tasks for the practitioner.

Shared office suites also offer unified services, such as a receptionist who will answer your phone with your company name. They also provide conference rooms, technology connections, fax and mail services, and many other standard services available to larger firms at a much reduced price. An example of this service is HQ (http://www.hq.com), with office suites all over the country.

Finally, consider outsourcing your legal research and writing. Many lawyers market themselves exclusively for these services. Lisa Solomon (http://www.questionoflaw.net), a New York attorney, concentrates her work in legal research and writing for attorneys. Having such tasks handled by an outside service, properly pre-approved by the client of course, can free up your time to handle other tasks.

Caveat Emptor

There are some cautions to these approaches, however. Never forget your ethical responsibilities and your obligations to your client. Again, this is obvious, but where larger firms have committees to handle ethical issues and sophisticated software and staff to run checks for the remotest of conflicts, the solo or small firm lawyer must dig into his/her negligible available time and perform these same tasks at an equally proficient level.

Since you have so many hats on your hat rack as a solo or small firm attorney, you need to always keep ethics and client responsibilities on your mind. It can be maddening because the normal response is, "I don't have time to do all this." But your cry will likely go unheard because you have chosen the size and nature of your practice.

The final, and perhaps most important, tip I can offer is that you manage the number of clients and cases you accept. You can easily fall into the trap of thinking, more clients equals more revenue and I can feed my family next month. However, if you neglect (hence the root of the term negligence) one client, it can ruin all that hard work you've put into everything else. By soiling one hat, you may need to take your entire hat collection to the dry cleaners.

As a friend of mine succinctly put it, "Run your practice; don't let your practice run you." Now take off your hats and go home.

Part II

Finding the Right Fit for Law Office Staff

There's no one-size-fits-all solution to staff in the law office. No longer does the one secretary per lawyer rule apply. Law office staff can be shared, rented, or even outsourced.

3 Suite Alternatives to Staffing

by David J. Abeshouse

Welcome to the "contrarian" chapter of this book. Here, we discuss a particular set of commercial tools designed to allow you to work without staff of your own in a setting that has unique appeal to many practitioners.

This is not a "virtual assistant" or other remote helper; rather, it is an overall office concept, with several variable components, that permits you to customize your arrangements to suit your needs and retain a level of flexibility absent in most other solutions. Indeed, you even can morph in a nanosecond from unstaffed to staffed in this setting, so perhaps it's not all that contrarian after all.

This concept goes by many names, including executive office suites (EOS), instant offices, business centers, and serviced offices; it encompasses numerous variations, including short- and long-term office rental, virtual offices, corporate identity or image programs, and network access—flexibility is a key element. We'll explore the principal options and focus on staffing aspects as well.

The Basics

In the typical EOS office situation where you are physically present (as contrasted with, for example, a "virtual office" setting, described later), you (as tenant/client) enter into a standard form agreement with the EOS (as landlord/services provider) for a short or medium term. These range generally from three months to two years; renewal options are available and some tenants remain for many years.

The agreement encompasses the lease of the designated office space (for one or more private offices, the space configuration of which may be flexible) as well as the provision of included services, and the offer of additional available service menu items. Typical basic services include "meet-and-greet" reception and personalized telephone screening); mail distribution and postage machines; broadband T-1 lines; phone (with handsets and voicemail) and fax lines; basic office furniture; building directory listing; security; office cleaning services; coffee and basic kitchen service; fax and photocopying machine usage at a cost per page; conference room access (some arrangements have a set number of hours per month built into the agreement, after which you pay on a usage basis; others are based strictly on usage charges); parking; and on-site center management personnel who can triage any issues. Providers usually charge an initial set-up fee, fixed monthly charges for rent and basic services, and separate charges for consumption of additional products and services.

Some Nuances and Add-Ons

Some providers offer expanded services, such as:

- Tech facilities such as videoconferencing and other audio-visual equipment and services) which otherwise may be prohibitively expensive for a solo.
- Bundled/pre-paid or by-the-hour or day conference room usage. Some providers have customizable meeting rooms and training rooms, or at least several rooms of varying size and capacity.
- Access to other centers nationwide or worldwide within a given company or network. Some providers have many hundreds of

centers in numerous countries; others use reciprocal arrangements.

- The option to add-on more office space either permanently or on a daily as-needed basis.
- Health club membership, often within the building.

Staffing Substitutes

EOS facilities often promote themselves as "serviced offices," with a built-in menu of physical features as well as services provided by employees of the facility. Some of the principal service components available include:

- Receptionist services, as already mentioned. This one service alone saves considerable employment cost, usually equivalent to or exceeding the cost of the EOS tenant's annual office rent.
- Postal mail and overnight mail. EOS staff will organize and distribute mail to each tenant and also can send your mail and packages, billing you for postage and time charges. Some business centers have discount arrangements with overnight delivery providers; some charge a premium for postage and mailing.
- Word processing, spreadsheets, mail merges, filing, and other secretarial tasks.
- Catering. Employees of the EOS facility will, for a flat charge or an hourly fee, arrange all of your office catering needs, from a business lunch for six to an evening on-site reception for dozens.
- Information technology and computer-related services, either through on-site staff or on-call.
- Office management tasks such as office product purchasing services and discounts (often through arrangements with companies such as RIM-Blackberry or telecom providers, FedEx or UPS, Staples or Office Depot).

Fundamentally, if your only employee would be performing these tasks, and having somewhat less direct control over the worker does not concern you, EOS staffing can save the solo or small firm lawyer much money, as well as the headaches of responsibility for employment withholdings and other administrative matters. The EOS tenant also does not have to engage in the hiring and firing process (which is mostly a good thing, although again it means relinquishing a measure of control). The economic model works very well in certain circumstances.

Consider the example of the law practice that might otherwise hire one full-time employee to serve as receptionist and also do fill-in work in various other capacities, such as mail, word processing, ordering lunch, and buying office supplies, up to 10 hours per week. This employee in a major metropolitan suburban area might command a salary of nearly $30,000 per year, plus benefits, additional office space, and computer, all likely totaling over $40,000 per year. However, these services might add only $500 per month ($6,000 per year) to the monthly rent relative to a traditional, unserviced office setting, and the additional several hours per week of EOS staff time charges might amount to another $1,000 per month (40 hours x $25/hour). Thus, by paying a differential of about $1,500 per month (the extra $6,000 per year for office cost plus the additional $12,000 per year for EOS staff charges, totaling $18,000 per year), the practice saves well over $20,000 per year, relative to the $40,000 cost of the employee. If the usage of EOS employees is less than 10 hours per week, the savings are even greater; some practices do not use EOS staff at all, thereby saving an additional $12,000 per year in our example. Moreover, this calculus does not account for the savings in the cost of office management services, some of which inherently are built into the basic agreement for physical office space.

However, once you have more than one or two on-site employees, the cost advantage of the EOS system usually vanishes quickly, unless none of your employees functions in the capacities filled by the EOS staff. Thus, if you hire only associate lawyers, the EOS model likely will work until you have more than two associates, depending on space utilization; if you hire an administrative or secretarial employee, the EOS advantage disappears more rapidly.

Alternative Versions

Through a virtual office arrangement, the solo or small firm can reap the advantages of attaching a prime business address to the practice, including phone and mail handling, without having to pay premium space rent rates. These arrangements also may be termed "corporate image" or "corporate identity" programs. They allow a firm to maintain a local presence without committing to a particular physical location, and are ideal for start-ups. Many home-based lawyers use this format, particularly those in potentially sensitive areas of practice such as criminal law and matrimonial law, to shield their homes from clients. Available services include mail collection and forwarding; use of a prestigious office address; access to conference rooms and office space as needed; use of administrative staff as needed; receptionist services, including screening and paging, as well as call-forwarding; kitchen/catering; audio-visual equipment; and building lobby listing. Additional levels of services are available from a menu of options, each at a set (or sometimes negotiable) price; some providers will "unbundle" services to allow you to pick and choose which elements are included in your customized plan. Among the options are:

- "Network access" provides you with use of the provider's branch offices while you are on the road. Business lounges, conference rooms, training rooms, day offices, and the associated services may be accessed through this system. Depending on the provider, access ranges from regional to nationwide to global.
- "Hot-desking" is for mobile or flextime employees, who can rotate among standardized workstations. This program can reduce the cost of space per person and increase desk utilization by placing multiple paralegals, secretaries, or others at one desk, depending on their schedules.
- The "cubes" concept allows a firm to grow one workstation at a time with self-contained, dedicated cubicles outfitted with equipment and furniture, a cost-effective solution for employees who require individual work areas.

Other less formalized but in many ways similar alternatives exist. Solos and small firm lawyers may rent office space from an entrepreneurial lawyer or firm that owns or rents a suite of offices and then sublets out individual offices (providing an EOS-style menu of attached services such as conference room usage, kitchen facilities, fax and photocopy machine usage, and the like). You may decide that you want to be the one who organizes such an arrangement in an effort to achieve "free rent" and perhaps a modest profit. More commonly, an existing law or other professional services firm may have an extra office or two to rent out, and may permit the tenant/sub-tenant to use office equipment and reception services. In either of these situations, there may be greater concerns about maintaining professional confidentiality, due to the proximity to and sharing of equipment with others. However, more personalized and flexible services may be available, depending on the approach of the suite operator.

Good Prospects

For whom might these officing solutions be attractive?

- Solo practitioners
- Small law firms with no more than four people
- Home-based firms wanting a virtual office or "corporate identity"
- Small branch offices of large law firms
- Law firms in transition, awaiting build-out of their new office space, for a period of a few months
- Lawyers needing office space immediately, without time to seek out traditional space opportunities, negotiate with a landlord, and set up the new space
- Lawyers or firms "testing the waters" in a particular location
- Law firms undergoing rapid growth, for temporary expansion space
- Seasonal practitioners such as those with a tax practice, who might need offices only for a few months each year—so-called "project offices"
- Mobile professionals
- Part-time or intermittent practitioners, who need use of an office only one or two days per week, or a set number of hours per month
- Those interested in emergency preparedness planning—maintaining several geographically disparate business locations can aid in times of natural disaster, attack, or other crisis

- Absentee owners. Michael Gerber, in his wildly successful book, *The E-Myth Revisited*, suggests that many business owners would benefit by moving their own office several blocks away from headquarters; the EOS setting might provide these business owners and executives with the necessary buffer.

Benefits: The Not-So-Tangible

Beyond the advantages already discussed, EOS centers also afford tenants the opportunity to grow their businesses by taking advantage of what often amounts to a business incubator: fellow tenants or suitemates may be prospective clients or at least possible sources of clients and referrals. Some EOS centers have many dozens of companies all "officed" in close proximity on one or two contiguous floors of a building. As tenants come to know their neighbors, they find that they can do business together.

EOS centers also provide social advantages. This is particularly so for solos or small firms with few or no staff. In contrast to a home office or a standalone office, EOS tenants usually can find an opportunity for a conversation with EOS employees or other tenants in the hallways, kitchen, or other common areas. Many EOS providers organize periodic gatherings and events around holidays and other opportunities (e.g., Halloween treats or Valentine's Day sweets in Conference Room B from 2:30 to 4:30 p.m.) so that tenants can meet and get to know each other, building a sense of community.

The Downside

Tenants or clients of executive office suites typically pay higher rental per square foot than do traditional tenants, but they receive added services that would cost more otherwise. This becomes a detriment only once you start to ramp up your need for additional space, usually due to staffing, for two related reasons: You're paying for reception and related services built-in to your contract cost, and you're paying a relatively high cost per square foot. Although this might make sense for a single office or even perhaps two, few tenant/clients stay at an EOS after they grow to the point where they need more than two or three offices, because they essentially are double-paying for the services (unless they negotiate and receive a volume discount). At that point, absent a price break, they probably can save money and exercise more control over their own destinies by having their own staff answer the phones, and by not paying redundantly for reception and other services.

As noted, although you benefit from not having to engage in the time-consuming hiring and firing process, and all aspects of human resource management in between, you also relinquish control over the workers, as they are not your employees. The workability of the inherent compromise here depends on your level of reliance on these workers and on other aspects of your personality.

Some EOS facilities are designed and constructed to be readily adaptable to tenants' changing needs, even to the extent of space configurations. At these centers, walls easily can be moved to suit shifting requirements. Accordingly, they may be built from thin sheetrock, which, for a loud next-door neighbor, can be a poor sound buffer. Although this also can occur in non-EOS settings, it may be more prevalent in the EOS arena.

In the interest of uniformity, control, and desire not to discriminate against varying aesthetic tastes, EOS centers may impose more stringent rules about decorating offices (and in particular doors facing into public hallways) than a regular landlord might. This is a matter of taste and of how much you care about customizing your décor.

To EOS or Not to EOS: It's a Question

A simple Google search for EOS will reveal plenty of options in most communities. Some of the larger providers, with nationwide or even worldwide centers, include Regus/HQ, Alliance Business Centers, ReadyOffices, and Intelligent Office. Many smaller regional and local companies run similar operations. Some operations focus primarily on the legal profession (for example, Barrister Executive Suites, Inc. in California). As mentioned, some individual proprietors and small firms take on additional space and create their own micro versions of the EOS concept, in an entrepreneurial effort to defray rental or ownership expense and perhaps turn a modest profit. It's worth researching to see whether the local options might suit your needs.

The EOS concept is not right for everyone. You must determine whether the benefits and flexibility outweigh the costs and limitations from your perspective. Do you prefer to forge forward without staff of your own for the foreseeable future? Or do you plan to staff up rapidly? Do you want to experiment with a short-term arrangement before committing to a long-term solution? Or do you want to plant your roots and get settled? Are you in transition and need somewhere to land for six months or a year? Or are you in a stable situation? Do you want to open a branch office as a turnkey rather than start-from-scratch operation? Search the web, then visit a few EOS providers in your area and compare their offerings to the other alternatives that are attractive to you. Try to speak with some of the tenants/clients of the provider to ask about their experiences and opinions. Only then will you be able to decide for yourself whether suites suit you best.

4

To Rent or to Employ: That Is the Question

by Jeffrey Allen

When I was younger and in a law partnership, our partnership had employees. We employed lawyers. We employed secretaries. We employed an office manager. We employed a receptionist. We employed paralegals. We even had an employed messenger/process server. As employers, we had all the headaches that come with the employment of employees. We had the "who do you hire" headaches. We had the "how much salary" headaches. We had the "retirement plan" headaches. We had the "how much vacation time" headaches. We had the "what about a raise" headaches. We had the "what about a bonus" headaches. We had the "how do you figure out who to fire" headaches. We had the "fringe benefit" headaches. We had the "what medical plan" headaches. We even had some employees that just gave us headaches.

We considered ourselves a small law firm even though we had as many as eight lawyers. Because we took on cases with larger firms on the other side, we frequently worked against firms substantially larger in size than our own. I have seen technology as a great equalizer for many years and have firmly entrenched myself at the leading edge of technological advancement and evolution in the practice of law.

Technology had created serious issues in the old partnership. I pushed for investment in new technology, believing that it would enable us as a smaller firm to compete successfully with larger firms and that it would enable us to run the practice more efficiently. My partners did not like the idea of making substantial investments in technology. They took the attitude that if we had something that worked, we should continue with it rather than chance something that might work better or worse. One partner expressed a clear preference for investing in additional personnel and more benefits for the existing personnel instead of in new technology, creating a polarity that invaded all of our discussions as to the operation of the firm.

In 1996, my partners and I, having managed to give each other several headaches that had little, if anything, to do with our employees, decided to end our partnership and go our separate ways. Interestingly, I quickly found that not having partners cured a lot of my headaches. It also gave me the opportunity to create a new structure for my law practice, based on a sole proprietorship model. I call it a sole proprietorship rather than a solo practice as I do have one lawyer who works for me, so I do not have a true solo practice. Incidentally, that one lawyer has been with me for almost 20 years, and I do employ her. She is the only person on my payroll, other than my wife, who comes in to help once in a while.

Because my partners and I set a date about four months out as the termination date for our partnership, I had some time to think about how I wanted to organize my new office structure. I wanted to set my new office up to run smoothly. I wanted efficiency both in the actual practice and in the cost of operations. I have long recognized that the level of elasticity of legal fees had finite limits and have always tried to provide excellent service to my clients, while keeping the cost of my services in a range that allowed my clients to afford them, but that still covered my expenses and provided me with a reasonable income. I did not want to change that perspective in my new office. I wanted to set the office up to facilitate achievement of those ends.

Issues of employee pay and benefits (to say nothing of the number of support personnel we had) posed many problems for the partnership. Some of them, such as terminating the 401(k) plan, lasted some time after the partnership ended as a result of the fact that we had lost track of some former employees, who had contributed to the plan but not transferred their retirement funds after leaving their jobs at our firm. I wanted to avoid going back to the same place in my new office.

Solving the Staffing Conundrum

I took several steps to reduce expenses and make the office run more efficiently. One of those steps, perhaps the most important economically, was the decision not to employ most of my own support personnel.

I do not have any employed secretarial help. I do not have an employed receptionist. I do not have an employed bookkeeper. For the last 10 years, I have "rented" secretarial and clerical help on an "as needed" basis. In the last few years, I have found other means of getting some of my work done in order to allow me to reduce the amount of the support time I needed to rent on a day-to-day basis. The end result: greater efficiency at lower cost.

I have found that renting employees offers significant advantages over fully employing all support staff personnel:

1. I can add additional help with relative ease whenever I need it, even if just for a temporary situation.
2. I can easily and relatively painlessly reduce staff if the situation warrants. All it takes is a phone call to the agency that supplies me with personnel, and I have reduced my expenses by not using a part of the rented support staff or by reducing the time that I rent support personnel.
3. I substantially reduce or avoid the cost of dealing with vacations and other fringe benefits.
4. I substantially reduce or avoid the time and effort required on an administrative level to deal with vacations, insurance, retirement plans and other fringe benefits.

Dictating and Transcription

Recent developments have made it even easier for me to get my secretarial needs covered. I discovered the wonders of digital dictation and no longer use my micro-cassette dictation equipment. I consider cassettes of all sizes as out of date as a manual typewriter. I now use a digital recording device for dictation. Using the digital recorder affords me considerable freedom and flexibility that I did not have with the older micro-cassette technology.

Cassette-based technology (using a tape for recording dictation) works fine as long as the person doing dictation and the person doing transcription both work in the same location. While one could hire an outside transcription service and deliver the tape to the service, that procedure would likely impose a significant inefficiency on the office.

With digital technology, I can record at the office, at home, or on the road and transfer the file for transcription electronically and instantaneously. The transfer can go to a secretary in my office or to an outside transcription service. Many transcription services provide staffing on a 24/7 basis, including over most holidays, increasing the flexibility even more. By way of example, I am working on this manuscript on the Sunday of Labor Day weekend. On Tuesday, I have to leave by 10 a.m. to make an out of town exp parte court appearance to apply for a Temporary Restraining Order and an Order to Show Cause Why Preliminary Injunction Should Not Be Granted. I had a busy week last week and did not get everything done for the appearance. I finished the complaint and the required declarations and proposed orders, but did not finish the Memorandum of Points and Authorities. I took the research and file home with me, along with my digital recorder. I spent some time on Saturday afternoon working on the memorandum, but did not finish it before I left to take my wife out to dinner and a movie. After we got home, I finished dictating the memorandum. I took the memory card out of the recorder, plugged it into my computer, and uploaded the file to the transcription service I use at around midnight, Pacific time. I will get it back, finalize it, and leave for my appearance on Tuesday. Using rented support or permanent, employed staff, I would have had to bring someone in over the holiday weekend to get it done, or type it myself.

For some time now, I have used a transcription service that will transcribe my work for me within 24 hours. They guarantee me a 24-hour turnaround and, for a surcharge, offer expedited service when I need it. In fact, the service that I use has proven quite good and I usually get my work back in less than 24 hours. Often I will upload files at 6 p.m. and download my work mid-day the next day. I have found that the accuracy of the service's production rivals that of a secretary in my office, but I only pay for the time spent typing. As a result, the cost of my production has significantly decreased.

As a result of the arrangements I have with the transcription service, the same typists generally do my work, thereby acquiring some familiarity with my style of dictation and improving the accuracy of the work. The use of the transcription service affords me almost complete flexibility. If I turn out a lot of dictation one day, they simply have another transcriber pick some of it up. If I have a trial or, for some other reason, do not turn out a lot of dictation, I do not pay for time I do not use or for a permanent employee to work on their personal matters or surf the net. If I end up doing the dictation in the evening, I can transmit it for transcription from home or, for that matter, anywhere else as long as I have a computer and an Internet connection. I could not easily achieve that level of flexibility with rented support or a full-time staff of employees. In that situation, I would have to look at renting or hiring additional help or paying overtime to employees when I have an abundance of work and paying salaries to employees when they have little or nothing to do.

The use of the transcription service has substantially reduced the cost of producing my work. I have tracked a reduction of more than 30 percent as a result of that approach. The disadvantage of this approach is that I have less support staff available to handle some of the mundane tasks required to keep a law office running. I have not noticed that this created a significant problem for me or takes me away from productive work enough to outweigh the savings generated by this approach.

The evolution of voice-recognition software offers yet another way to inexpensively convert dictation to word-processed text. If you spend some time with the current iteration of Dragon Naturally Speaking, it provides very good conversion of words to text. It costs even less than a transcription service as you buy the program once, make any necessary hardware expenditures, and then keep using it.

The Money Angle

The savings I have realized result from a combination of not paying salary for support staff time that I do not need and saving on fringe benefits associated with full-time employees.

Although I pay a premium to the agency that provides me with support staff over what the service pays its workers, the cost that I incur for such rented staff does not run as high as what I would pay in salary and benefits to have a staff of full-time employees.

Salaries for legal secretaries and paralegals have increased significantly in recent years. Additionally, the cost of fringe benefits, particularly medical/dental insurance, has also skyrocketed. Salaries for experienced legal secretaries in my area generally fall into the $50,000 to $60,000 a year range, augmented, of course, by the annual holiday bonus, vacation, medical benefits, and often a retirement program. An employer pays the salary of a full-time employee in sickness and in health, during times of work and times of vacation.

Full-time employees generally expect that they will get paid vacation time. Generally, after several years of work, they expect that their vacation time will increase from a week or two to three or four weeks. When an employee takes off for vacation, the employer continues to pay the employee's salary; the employer also pays benefit expenses for the vacationing employee. While employees take vacation time, they do not perform the work that they would normally do in the office. Accordingly, the employer gets to pay an employee's salary and associated benefits for vacation time and also incurs the additional expense of hiring temporary personnel to do the vacationing employee's work or pay other employees overtime to try to cover the additional work. Rented employees and/or the outsourcing of transcription services avoids those expenses entirely or, at least, reduces them to the extent that you substitute rented support staff or outsource your transcription.

Fringe benefits have grown more and more expensive over time. One of the fastest growing fringe benefits is medical/dental insurance. My insurance broker recently advised me that the monthly premium for the Blue Cross PPO medical insurance plan we had in our office will increase to over $1,100 per person. Certainly, insurance companies offer less expensive plans, but, generally speaking, lower premiums equate to lower benefits. While you may feel that it makes sense to pay for a less expensive plan for your employees, remember that you also get the lower benefits of the less expensive medical plans for yourself and your family. Such costs add up quickly. For example, medical insurance under our current plan for two more full-time employees would cost an additional $2,200 per month or over $26,000 per year.

Another advantage of not having employees relates to the adoption of retirement plans. Some time ago I was informed that under applicable law, if the owner(s) of a business establish a retirement plan, they must allow employees to participate in it in most cases, after a qualifying period. As the owner of a business, I could not set up a retirement plan for myself without allowing employees to participate and making contributions for all of my employees. By renting support staff, I enabled the creation of a retirement plan for my one full-time employee and myself without having to contribute to the retirement plans of other employees.

What to Look for in Rented Staff

I will take a moment to talk about some of the things you need to watch for if you intend to go this route. First, if you want to use rented support staff in your own office, you will need to locate a reliable agency to provide workers to you. In any major metropolitan area, you will likely find several agencies that provide such services. In more rural areas, you may find it harder to locate agencies that do this, let alone that do it well. You will need an agency that understands the level and quality of workers that you will require and the skill set(s) that workers will need to work for you successfully and satisfactorily. They will also need to have the ability to produce workers of the required caliber and with the required skill sets. Generally, you will not find what you want through temp agencies. You want to find an agency that works on providing long-term staffing to firms. You also want to make sure that you get a trial period with the personnel that they will provide. Sometimes a person just does not work out, and you want to be able to replace them easily. Some agencies will want an agreement for a minimum term; that, of course, reduces your flexibility somewhat. If you look around, you should be able to find an agency that will provide what you want on a long-term basis at an hourly rate. Depending on your workload, you may want to consider a long-term, part-time arrangement, such as three days per week or short workdays. Often you can find a worker who wants to work such a schedule, but will come in on an extra day or stay longer from time to time, should the need arise. Such an arrangement improves your flexibility.

Do not think that the rental of employees means that you will have new people every few weeks or even every few months. While that can happen, if you choose the agency carefully, you can do much better. I have rented secretaries and receptionists who have stayed with me up to two years. I still have the same bookkeeper that I had when I started the sole proprietorship. He also worked as the bookkeeper for the partnership. I have rented his services for almost 11years as a sole proprietor and several more as a partner in the old partnership.

If you choose to outsource transcription, you will find more and more vendors available to provide that service. In fact, at a recent trade show, I ran into representatives of several such operations, including some agencies that have their transcription services outsourced offshore as a cost-savings device. I will leave it to you to decide whether that will work for you. Under any circumstances, check out the timing, delivery, and costs of the services you consider. You will likely get better results if your work gets done by the same typist(s) on a regular basis than otherwise. Explore the availability of that type of coordination with a potential vendor.

Remember, that nothing precludes you from trying out a few service providers to see how you like working with them. Similarly, nothing prevents you from moving from one service provider to another in order to find the structure that works best for your organization.

5

Kellie: Our Special Employee

by Ted A. Waggoner

Our small law office generates five to 10 pounds of recyclable paper every day. In the mid-1980s we stopped burning this paper and began shredding and recycling. Whenever a secretary had a few extra moments, she would feed the paper through the personal-sized paper shredder. The shredded paper was then bagged and donated to the local recycling center.

After several months, it became obvious that this process was not working well, and so I hired my teenage daughter to come in on occasional Saturday mornings and shred. There was some awkwardness around this, and we discussed the need for confidentiality about anything that she might see. We never had a problem. During her high school years, between athletic events, late Friday nights, and time preparing for college, the stack of unshredded paper grew.

We then hired another girl from the neighborhood to help us, also an honor student, capable of understanding issues of confidentiality, but since she was not a partner's child, she turned out to be even less willing to show up regularly to feed paper into the throat of the now larger paper shredder.

As we were trying to decide how to handle the growing mounds of paper, the local high school special education teacher dropped in one day and asked if there were any jobs in the law office that would be appropriate for a Down Syndrome student he had. After a few questions about the capability of the student to read, comprehend, and remember legal issues—or at least the names of clients—as well as questions about the student's ability to be trained on shredding machinery, we agreed to try Kellie for the job.

The school was pleased that we were willing to consider training Kellie and to offer her some job skills. She came two days a week, for two hours each time. The school provided an aide to supervise Kellie every day. The aide was also advised about the issues of confidentiality, and accepted the responsibility of supervision.

We offered to pay the minimum wage for Kellie's services, which the school rejected under the program. We taught Kellie to maintain a record of her hours and paid her for the time she spent, as a Christmas bonus (with a wink and nod from the school). After a few weeks Kellie began to understand the operation of the paper shredder, how to clear clogs, and the need to wear safe clothing every time she came to work. She brought a CD player and sang along with the music.

For several months after Kellie began working, the aide would come along and stay in the building, but not always at Kellie's elbow. Kellie is now 21 and is in her fourth year of working as a valued member of our firm. She is paid above the minimum wage and she has learned a bit about taxes. She now has the local public transportation system deliver her to work two days a week for about two hours at a time and is able to maintain the recycling of the materials we produce.

The aide stopped coming more than a year ago, and Kellie's independence keeps growing month by month. She now works at the local Blockbuster store as well as at the office. Kellie's employment has been a positive and rewarding experience for the office as well as for Kellie. You might want to explore a similar program.

Outsourcing Legal Research and Writing Projects

6

by Lisa Solomon

Why Outsource Your Legal Research and Writing Projects

Lawyers outsource legal research and writing projects for a variety of reasons. One primary reason is time: unfortunately, lawyers are not always in control of their own schedules. Deadlines—whether set by statute, court rule, or judicial fiat—are ever present.

While a large firm might simply pull an associate from one matter to work on another, more pressing, case, small firms and solo practitioners usually don't have that luxury. This makes small firms and solos particularly vulnerable to periodic "workload overload."

Some tasks—such as trials, client meetings, and rain-making—demand your personal attention; others, such as legal research and writing, do not. Outsourcing enables you to weather particularly busy periods without having to hire an employee or face time pressures that lead to lawyer stress and burnout.

Another benefit of outsourcing legal research and writing on an as-needed basis is cost. Hiring an associate requires a significant investment in both time and money. When you outsource legal research and writing projects, you pay only for the time it takes to complete the project, but when you hire an employee, you immediately add to your fixed expenses. Searching for and training a new associate (particularly a junior-level associate) is time-consuming. Your practice may be busy enough to benefit from project-based outsourcing, but not busy enough to not support another employee. Outsourcing is a wise use of your firm's resources that can increase profitability.

Hiring an associate has other downsides that can be avoided by retaining an independent contractor to assist you with your research and writing needs. An employee adds to your administrative burdens, especially if you are a solo practitioner. Your malpractice rates will rise and you will be subject to all the financial and legal responsibilities that accompany "employer" status. Retaining an independent contractor is much less complicated, both initially and on an ongoing basis.

In fact, outsourcing legal research and writing projects can help your firm's bottom line. With one or two exceptions, all of the bar associations that have addressed the issue—including, most notably, the ABA[1]—have determined that a lawyer may charge the client a premium or reasonable measure of profit in excess of the research and writing provider's cost to the lawyer, as long as the total charges to the client are reasonable.[2] Regardless of whether or not you choose to charge your client more than you pay for legal research and writing services, outsourcing is still cost-effective for your client, since even a

---

1. *See* ABA Formal Op. 08-451 (Lawyer's Obligations When Outsourcing Legal and Nonlegal Support Services), ABA Formal Op. 00-420 (Surcharge to Client for Use of a Contract Lawyer), ABA Formal Op 89-256 (Temporary Lawyers).

2. The exceptions are the Maryland Bar Association and the Professional Ethics Committee for the State Bar of Texas. However, the Maryland Bar Association did not give any reason or cite any rule in support of the position it expressed in Md. Bar Assoc. Ethics Comm. Op 92-19 (1992), and the reasoning of the Professional Ethics Committee for the State Bar of Texas in Opinion 577 (March 2007) is questionable. *See* Corey L. Marrs, *Being a Contract Lawyer and How the Bar Does Not Want You to Hire Me*, NEWS FOR THE BAR (Litigation Section of the State Bar of Texas, Fall 2007).

rate that includes a reasonable profit to you will generally be lower than your own hourly rate.

Moreover, a lawyer who concentrates in legal research and writing can often accomplish those jobs more efficiently than a busy practitioner who may not be as familiar with the available resources or as experienced in searching large databases for sometimes elusive answers. You may already outsource other tasks to independent professionals, such as private investigators, in order to benefit from their expertise. Outsourcing frees you to use your valuable time in a way that is most efficient for you and your clients.

Finally, some lawyers simply like doing "outside" work—such as trials, depositions, and client meetings—more than "inside" work, such as legal research and writing. Outsourcing frees you to do those tasks that you find most personally and professionally rewarding.

What Types of Legal Research and Writing Projects Can Be Outsourced?

It is not always necessary to outsource an entire legal research and writing project. On one end of the spectrum, you may have already researched the issues and drafted a brief, but need someone to edit your work. Or you may need help with research, but want to write a brief or opinion letter yourself. Or you may prefer to delegate primary responsibility for an entire large project—including the preparation of a record on appeal, legal research, and brief writing—to your provider (working under your ultimate supervision, of course). Look for a provider who will accommodate your preferred work style.

Outsourcing legal research and writing is not just for litigators. Although there are more opportunities for litigators to outsource legal research and writing work on an ongoing basis, transactional lawyers can also benefit from working with independent providers. For example, a lawyer who is drafting a contract that will be used by a business client with outlets in many states may want to know how courts in those jurisdictions will construe a particular contract provision. Or a real estate practitioner may agree to handle a litigation matter arising from a failed deal (as an accommodation to the client), but may be rusty when it comes to legal research and brief writing.

Even if you are handling a case on a contingency basis and will be absorbing the provider's fees yourself, it may still make sense to work with an independent legal research and writing services provider. Hiring a provider to work on a low-value case frees you up to devote more time to higher-value cases; conversely, an experienced provider can offer critical legal research and writing assistance in a high-value case. A legal research and writing provider can even help you decide whether or not to accept a contingency case by examining issues you have identified at the outset (such as whether a statute of limitations was tolled based on the facts of the case) or by performing a jury verdict search.

Small firms and solo practitioners in particular can benefit from the fresh perspective and critical eye that an outside researcher/writer can bring to a case. For example, sometimes it is difficult to dispassionately evaluate legal issues in a case to which you have already committed significant resources; other times an issue arises that is outside your expertise. Although chatting informally with a colleague about your case may help point you in the right direction, a legal research and writing services provider who is familiar with all of the relevant facts and has read the applicable cases and statutes will be able to analyze the issues more closely.

How to Find a Legal Research and Writing Services Provider

The process of finding the right legal research and writing services provider is no different from finding the right carpenter to build a backyard deck or IT professional to oversee your office's computer network—the best place to start is with personal recommendations. Since outsourcing legal research and writing projects has become more common over the past few years, it's likely that a colleague can recommend someone.

If the referral avenue leads to a dead end, your next step should be a Web search. Since it is not necessary for the provider you hire to be licensed in the jurisdiction in which you are admitted or where the matter is venued, the pool of available providers will be fairly broad.

Just as law firms range from one lawyer to thousands, some legal research and writing services providers are solos, while others are larger companies. If you are considering retaining a larger firm, note whether the company's Web site identifies the company's principals (even if it doesn't identify all the researchers).

Whether you find a provider through a personal referral or a Web search, you should review some writing samples (including a sample of the type of document—such as a summary judgment brief or internal memo—that you expect the provider to draft) to ensure that the provider's writing ability meets your standards.

You should also closely examine the provider's Web site. Is it well-written and free of grammatical and typographical errors? Look for testimonials on the provider's Web site from named clients; if there are no testimonials, make sure to obtain and follow up on references.

What to Look for in a Legal Research and Writing Services Provider

Generally, a legal research and writing services provider will not become counsel of record for your client; rather, the provider will be working under your general supervision as a subcontractor to you. Therefore, it is not necessary for the provider to be licensed in your state.

A dedicated research and writing services provider should have his or her own legal research subscription plan (or access to a well-stocked law library) that includes all of the materials that you would want access to if you were doing the research yourself. Except in extraordinary circumstances or as otherwise agreed in advance, your provider should not bill you for the cost of accessing any databases or materials that are relevant to the legal issues involved.

For risk management purposes, make sure your provider carries malpractice or errors and omissions insurance. Although your malpractice policy will most likely cover you for work performed by an independent legal research and writing provider, you (or your insurance company) may wish to seek indemnification from the provider.

Best Practices for Working with a Legal Research and Writing Services Provider

As with any other type of contract, it is wise to have a written agreement with your provider. At a minimum, the agreement should include provisions: (1) requiring the provider to maintain the confidentiality of any and all client information the provider learns while working on matters for you, to the same extent as if the provider had an attorney-client relationship with your clients; (2) establishing the basis for and amount of payment to the provider (e.g., $150 per hour or $3,000 to research and draft a particular motion); (3) addressing how disbursements will be handled (for example, will the provider advance expenses for appellate printing, or will you pay those expenses directly?); and (4) setting forth the choice of law and forum in the event that a dispute arises.

If the provider is billing on an hourly basis, you may want to receive regular progress reports (for example, you may ask that the provider discuss the project's status with you at the 10-hour mark). You can also instruct the provider not to spend more than a certain amount of time on a project. Although such an approach will make the provider's total fees more predictable, the project may not be completed within the allotted time. (To ameliorate this risk, you may wish to negotiate a flat fee for the entire project.) Once you have established a relationship with a provider who has demonstrated the ability to complete projects to your standards in a timely and efficient manner, you may find it unnecessary to use these monitoring techniques.

You may enter into a broad agreement designed to set the ground rules for work on an unlimited number of current and future matters or a more limited agreement that applies only to one matter. If you enter into a broad agreement, make sure that you specify the scope of each particular project in writing at the outset of the project.

A critical part of establishing a project's scope is to clearly define the research issues. It is also important, however, to be open to your provider's input, since initial research may sometimes enable the provider to identify other issues that impact your case. Your provider should bring these issues to your attention and obtain express authorization to go beyond the initial project scope before proceeding.

The give-and-take extends to the writing process. It's wise to discuss major substantive changes to a document your provider has drafted, since drafting decisions are premised on the provider's analysis of the issues. Any divergence between your analysis and/or conclusions and the provider's may indicate a weakness in the case that merits further exploration. Additionally, if you're working with an experienced writer, you will benefit from being open to his or her feedback on your writing style.

Although some legal research and writing services providers insist that the hiring attorney not reveal the identity of the ultimate client, it is much more efficient for solos and small firm lawyers to be able to freely share all information when working on an outsourced project than to have to redact documents. Assuming that you will be sharing all relevant information about each case with the services provider, you and the provider should treat conflicts issues as if the provider were an employee of your firm.

While you certainly can ask a provider to perform work at your office, the vast majority of providers do not work on-site. Free or cost-effective technologies, such as Basecamp (a turnkey intranet service) and YouSendIt.com (which allows you to send large files over the internet) allow you to easily collaborate on document-intensive projects (such as a summary judgment motion in a hotly contested case). Even if you end up sending hard copies of documents to your provider, the shipping cost will be far outweighed by the financial benefits both you and your clients can obtain by outsourcing legal research and writing projects.

The provider should be willing and able to deliver exactly the type of work product you need. On one project, you may only need the provider to e-mail you the relevant cases he or she has located; in another matter, you may ask the provider to draft a summary judgment motion. The provider should also be able to deliver results to you in your preferred word-processing format.

Other Ethical Issues in the Outsourcing Relationship

In addition to the issues of billing, conflicts and confidentiality that are briefly discussed above, other ethical considerations are relevant to the outsourcing relationship. One important issue is the hiring lawyer's duty to adequately supervise and oversee the provider's work. Although this chapter presumes that your provider is admitted in at least one U.S. jurisdiction, any provider who is not licensed in your jurisdiction will be considered a "non-lawyer" under your state's ethical rules. And, of course, even if you are working with a provider who is admitted in your jurisdiction, you retain the obligation to adequately supervise the provider—just as you would bear the responsibility to oversee and supervise an associate. (If you prefer not to maintain this responsibility, you may want to consider a referral or co-counsel relationship instead of an outsourcing relationship.)

Another question is whether you must disclose to the client your use of a legal research and writing services provider. Although, under ABA Op. 88-356, a hiring lawyer is not required to disclose the use of a contract lawyer or obtain the client's consent to such an arrangement where the contract lawyer is working under the direct supervision of a lawyer associated with the firm, disclosure is required if the contract lawyer is performing independent work for a client without the close supervision of a lawyer associated with the firm. Furthermore, many state and local bar associations have issued ethics opinions requiring disclosure under some circumstances, and others mandate disclosure under all circumstances. Thus, the safest route (particularly if you practice in a state that has not issued a governing ethics opinion) is to disclose, and obtain the client's consent to, your use of a research and writing specialist. If you will be billing an experienced provider's services to your client at a rate lower than your own, this process can actually be an opportunity to demonstrate your commitment to achieving the best possible result for the client at the lowest cost.

As long as the provider is not working on a contingent basis, you are not required to disclose the billing arrangements between you and the provider; in other words, you do not need to reveal the amount of profit you are making (assuming that you mark up the provider's bill). This position makes sense—after all, if an associate (i.e. your employee) was working on a client's matter, you would not be obliged to reveal the associate's salary to your client.

Part III

Your Staff, Your Team

Although additional staff would seem to make a lawyer's lot simpler and more lucrative, freeing lawyers to do what they do best—practicing law—the reality is that more employees mean more responsibilities: hiring, firing, supervising, and training that staff. Ethical issues abound for the specific tasks legal staff can and can't perform, and the buck stops with the lawyer. Generating revenue that meets the payroll simply isn't enough. The very elements that can make a law office successful—making a profit and effectively serving clients—can shatter expansion dreams. Although staff can help bring profit, clients, fame, and glory to lawyers, ineffective supervision can cost them money, lost clients, reputation, and even a license to practice. Simply practicing law isn't enough when lawyers become employers and small business owners.

Chapter 9: A Blueprint for Marketing with Staff
by Robert A. Kraft

Chapter 10: Care and Feeding of the Law Office Staff
by Jim Calloway

Chpater 11: Keys to Success: Leadership, Attorney-Staff Relations, and Simplified Action Planning
by Nancy Byerly Jones

Chapter 12: Motivating Lawyers and Employees in the Small Law Office
by Jim Karger

Support Staff— Opportunities and Challenges

7

by David Leffler

Support staff can be a great resource for lawyers; as they leave the non-legal work for their staff, lawyers work more efficiently, multiplying their effectiveness and the number of hours that they bill—but only if implemented correctly. The dark side of support staff is countless hours settling disputes amongst staff and between staff and lawyers, staff members who don't have the skills needed for the job, and lawyers unhappy because their work is not getting done.

Hiring

Hiring is where problems are avoided or can begin, based on hiring the procedures you either have or don't have in place. Fundamentally, what you want to know is, does the applicant have the right qualifications to work at your firm?

The two important qualifications are work history, to determine skills, and personality, to determine a fit with the culture of the law firm. Work history is obtained in three ways: resumé, interview, and independent investigation.

Resumé

The resumé is a two-dimensional object (literally) and will provide some, but not all, of what you need to know. Keep in mind that not everything on every resumé is 100 percent accurate, and some items are 100 percent fabrications, especially life experiences that are difficult to verify. If a college degree is important to you, then check with the college to verify that the applicant actually attended and graduated with the degree and in the year indicated. Even if a college degree is not important, if you discover that the applicant lied (or exaggerated) about any detail of his or her education or anything else on the resumé, consider if you really want to have this person working at your law firm. The best practice is to verify everything on the resumé of the person whom you've decided to hire.

Some details of the resumé that are not directly relevant to qualifications nevertheless may indicate good employee qualities. If the person lists that they have traveled around the globe, it can indicate a broader view on life that may enhance the work they will be doing at your firm. Starting a business in high school or college shows initiative and creativity, making it likely that this person is a "self-starter." Just do your best to find out whether he or she really did start up and operate a "retail refreshment beverage business" in high school or whether the applicant merely ran a lemonade stand for a few weeks one summer.

Interview

The interview is in some ways an odd process. On one hand you have the job seeker attempting to put his or her best foot forward, concealing anything that might reduce the odds of being hired. On the other hand, you have the employer attempting to break through any artifice to determine whether or not the applicant would make a good employee.

How do you break up this social logjam?

First, instead of sitting behind a desk directly facing the job applicant, arrange two chairs at right angles to each other without a desk, which will do wonders to loosen things up a bit, making it more likely that there will be a genuine exchange between you and the applicant.

Next, start the conversation about the weather, something bizarre your dog did as you left your home that morning, or anything else you can think of, as long as you are not violating any applicable federal or state laws that prohibit questions on certain topics, such as the applicant's marital status or children. This will relax the applicant, increasing the odds that you might have a real conversation, rather than a carefully scripted delivery of the applicant's best points.

There have been books written about how to conduct an employee interview, but permit me to provide you with two suggestions that will go a long way to making the interview a productive one. First, ask as many open-ended questions as possible. Rather than asking, "Did you like your last job?" ask, "What are some of the things you liked and didn't like at your last job?" Instead of getting a "yes" or "no" answer, you will get a more extensive reply that can help you get a better sense of the person.

Second, describe one or more real life scenarios that have or might occur at your law firm and ask how the applicant would deal with the situation. "A client shows up at the office for a meeting that they say has been scheduled with me, but I'm nowhere to be found. What do you do?" You may be surprised by some of the answers that you get. It certainly is not a good indication of his or her aptitude for the job if the applicant responds by giving you a blank stare.

Be sure to set up interviews with at least a dozen prospects, if you can line up that many. Why? First, because there will be some no shows. Second, the more people to whom you speak, the better sense you will get of what is out there (making you a better interviewer as the process continues) and the more likely it is that you will hire an employee that is well suited to your needs. You can do this in a way that minimizes the time involved by dedicating two afternoons (or mornings) to interviews. Hand the resumés to your assistant with the instructions to book interviews within specified time periods that you have blocked out. I find that blocking out 20 minutes for each interview is sufficient, allowing up to three interviews per hour. You can always call back your top choice or choices for a more extensive interview if needed.

Remember to deliver the basic information about the job to each applicant, such as the duties, hours, salary, and whether or not health insurance coverage or other benefits are included.

Independent Investigation

Twenty years ago, the only way to conduct an independent investigation was to hire a private investigator. This still is a valuable way to check on the background of an applicant, but it is expensive and today the Internet offers quite a bit at a much lower cost. However, if you are hiring someone for a key position, such as bookkeeper, I strongly recommend that you still hire a private investigation firm to do a thorough examination of the applicant, including a criminal background check.

The Internet offers a number of tools to check up on an applicant. First, there are the search engines. Google is what most people think of, but each search engine delivers at least a slightly different set of links, so it also pays to look at Yahoo (http://www.yahoo.com), Microsoft's Live Search (http://www.live.com), and Ask (http://www.ask.com), which recently got an upgrade and now presents information in a much more useful way than just the typical list of links. Or, if you really want to save some time, check out a meta-search engine, such as http://www.dogpile.com, which searches Google, Yahoo, Live, and Ask all in one search. Put quotes around a name to limit the returns to only the whole name and not returns that just have the first name "Robert" or "Susan."

Next you will want to check out the social networking sites such as Myspace (http://www.myspace.com) and Facebook (http://www.facebook.com), where you can often find photos of site members in very un-businesslike attire engaged in very un-businesslike activities. Also, check the more business-oriented social networking site LinkedIn (http://www.linkedin.com), where you may not find anything scandalous, but might find something that conflicts with or has been omitted from the applicant's resumé. Save yourself some time by using http://www.Wink.com, a search engine that specifically targets people by searching the public profiles on MySpace, Bebo, Friendster, LinkedIn, LiveSpaces, and other sources. Finally, if you really want to get deep into it, check out Craig Ball's (http://www.cybersleuthing.com), where you'll find all sorts of papers and links to other Webs sites to assist you in a deeper background search on the Internet.

Personality

An applicant may have all the qualifications necessary for your bio patent/immigration law practice, but might not be a good fit because of personality. The quiet types may not be comfortable in a firm where people yell down the hallway instead of using the intercom. If the applicant suffers from attention deficit disorder, your messy office may send him or her into a panic or perhaps cause him or her to make it neater than it's ever been. Consider asking questions during the interview that will expose potential conflicts by letting the interviewee know about the characteristics of your law firm that may affect comfort level. If nothing else, don't hide the fact that your office is messy or people regularly have loud conversations in the hallway. Let them see your office, warts and all. Even if the applicant says that he or she is comfortable with messy offices, he or she will find a reason not to return if in fact just the question made them dizzy and faint.

Now That You've Made the Hire

When you were growing up, was there ever a hot summer day when you were the only kid with an ice cream cone? I'm sure that you got a lot of attention and reasons you should share that ice cream cone, "I'm your friend" being one of the top reasons offered.

Now that you're all grown up and mature, sharing is not the ordeal that it once was—or is it? Walk into any busy law firm on a Friday afternoon and I bet that many of them are experiencing a tension similar to your childhood conflict many summers ago, except that now it is a fight over staff, not ice cream.

Playing Nice

The proper allocation of work to secretaries and paralegals is one of the most critical aspects in managing support staff. Each lawyer needs different degrees and types of support from the staff nd each has his or her own deadline. Unfortunately, in too many law firms there is little procedure as to how support staff is provided, other than when a staff member is initially assigned to a lawyer with the only instruction being, "Here's your assistant whom you'll be sharing with six other lawyers."

But a lack of procedure can often lead to turf wars over assistants, with the most senior lawyer winning, whether or not it makes sense from the point of view of an efficient allocation of firm resources. The senior partner might need someone to check flight schedules for a vacation he or she is planning in six months, but perhaps a greater priority should be given to motion papers due in court at 10 a.m. the next day.

So how do you develop a system to allocate staff resources so that everybody is happy, or at least that everyone's needs are attended to in a timely way? Here are some suggestions, but remember each office has its own particular needs, so use or adapt these suggestions in a way that makes sense for your office,

- Have one partner be the assignment partner reviewing staff duties at the beginning of each day. (Other partners can substitute for this job if the assignment partner is in court or at some other meeting that day.) This job can be rotated on an annual or semiannual basis among the partners.
- If you feel that more formality is required, create an assignment form that lawyers must fill out that describes (i) who is requested to do the work, (ii) the nature of the assignment, (iii) the deadline, (iv) any special needs to get the assignment done (equipment, outside vendors, travel, etc.), and (v) any other information that would be useful for your office operations. You may wish to limit this form to only those staff members who are "floaters" and not to assigned personnel.
- In a less formal system, lawyers gives their assignments to whomever they want if the office works on a pool system, or else to their assigned support staff. When a staff member determines that there is a conflict or overload, he or she goes to the assignment partner, who sorts it out. In any case, staff members should report what they are working on to the assignment partner with deadline requirements for each task; this will give the assignment partner an indication when one staff member is being overburdened and another's workload is lighter than the others.

- Maintain an electronic calendar system that permits anyone in the office to see computer both lawyer and staff vacations and other absences well in advance. Both support staff and lawyers should know these schedules, for when there are lawyers out this will free up staff for noncritical assignments that need to be done, such as file system updates, which involve reviewing client files for off-site storage, return to client, or destruction. These days there should be no excuse for not having an electronic calendar system, considering all the available inexpensive calendaring system software packages.
- Every so often have lawyers in the office provide a report on the strengths and weaknesses of support staff. If you wish, you can create a simple form that includes spaces for each staff member's greatest capabilities, areas where they are least capable, and suggestions for improvements and further training. In this way you will be alerted if there is a particular weakness in your staff that might be undermining the efficiency or abilities of the lawyers to produce a good work product.

Why Can't We All Just Get Along?

You've followed all of the above advice and have an assignment partner, forms, and a calendaring system, but you don't know what to do about the lawyer in your firm who refuses to work with anyone except his or her favorite secretary. Lawyers do grow attachments to certain staff members because they know their habits and how to deal with them.

It's hard to pry the lawyer away from his or her favorite staff person, so instead make it clear to that lawyer that he or she does not have exclusive use of that staff person. Also, that staff person doesn't have to do all of the work assigned by his or her biggest fan. Instead, the staff person can delegate out at least some of the work to other staff members, and then supervise the completion of the work. It will be up to the law firm management to establish which staff members can delegate work and to whom.

Then there's the opposite problem—a lawyer can't stand a particular support person and refuses to work with that person. One possible solution is to sit down with the lawyer to find out exactly what it is about this person that annoys him or her so much. Then limit the work that the lawyer gives this person to items that are least likely to create friction. So if the lawyer feels that a certain staff member can't type to save his or her own life, have that person do work other than typing, such as copying, scheduling appointments, and making follow up calls.

8

Finding, Training, and Retaining Law Firm Personnel

by Susan D. Goldstein

Finding skilled senior administrators, paralegals, contract negotiators, and legal secretaries is an ongoing issue for law firms and companies. However, recruiting resources are now more varied and plentiful. Advertising on Internet job-posting sites such as http://www.monster.com, http://www.vault.com and http://www.law.com presents the opportunity for a firm to reach a much broader pool of candidates than ever before. Law firms and companies can also take advantage of their own Web sites to advertise internal openings. The key to successful online recruiting, however, is to describe the position in the most explicit terms possible so that the human resources department is not flooded with resumes from unqualified candidates.

Advertising in local legal publications is an excellent way to reach regional candidates; for executive staff, also consider the *Wall Street Journal,* which has readers all over the country. Utilize internal resources—referral bonuses can yield positive results. When a lawyer laterals into your firm, always ask whether he or she wants to bring a secretary or paralegal. Hiring team members from the lawyer's previous firm can mean a smoother transition. A legal secretary or paralegal who joins the firm with a new lateral hire will be motivated to learn the systems, policies, and procedures that will help the lawyer to practice law more efficiently.

Another resource for hiring legal staff is outside recruiters. The best recruiters have proven track records of sourcing and placing competent legal staff and have worked with many top-tier law firms. Recruiters should be able to write thorough job descriptions for positions and should know which firms have the caliber of candidates to fit open positions. A good recruiter knows the culture and environment of your firm and is prepared to market your opening to the most appropriate candidates.

The advantage presented by outside recruiters is their knowledge of the marketplace. The fee is worth it because the recruiter is on top of the frequent changes in your legal community (for example, which partner just left a large firm and took significant clients, several associates, and support staff with him; or which lawyers who stayed behind might be nervous in the aftermath of the departure and could be well qualified for positions in your firm). How do you reach them? A good recruiter will know the person to call, when to call, and how to position your firm and the opportunity it presents. A good recruiter will be able to present offers in a way that will help candidates make the best decision.

Winnowing Out the Chaff

After a pool of candidates has been identified, a preliminary phone interview is useful to narrow the group to those individuals with the desired skill set. When contacting candidates to arrange a phone interview, let them know what questions will be asked: Why are they interested in the position, what skills will they bring, and what are their major strengths and weaknesses. With advance warning, candidates have the opportunity to consider the questions, inventory their work experience, and give considered responses. This is not the Spanish Inquisition—the goal of the phone screen is to support your interest in the candidate, not to trip them up with trick questions. Candidates who know in advance that they will be expected to describe their strengths and weaknesses will probably be more honest than if they are taken off guard by such a request.

During the interview process, candidates should meet not only with their immediate supervisor but also with senior members of the firm and support staff. Candidates interviewing for a secretarial position to a partner should meet with associates and paralegals who also work with the partner. Every potential new hire should meet with the managing partner, executive director, and senior members of the staff. The more people involved in the decision-making process, the better the chances are that you will hire a successful long-term employee.

Lateral attorney candidates should meet with the office administrator in addition to the attorneys. The administrator can share valuable information relating to firm culture, policies, and procedures that might not be covered in the attorney meetings. By offering candidates the chance to meet with representatives from both the professional and support staffs, the candidate will be better prepared to make a well-informed decision regarding your firm's opportunity.

Training Considerations

After you have hired a new secretary, paralegal, administrator, or lawyer, what should happen on his or her first day of employment? Send an introductory e-mail to everyone in the firm, containing a brief history of the new employee's work experience, pertinent personal facts, and the new employee's phone number and e-mail address. Some firm training programs include computer training and meetings with the benefits manager or human resources representative, records manager, MIS, office services, etc. A copy of the orientation schedule should be given to the new employee on the first day, along with the documents that need to be completed for payroll and medical benefits, a copy of the policy and procedures manual, and state/federal-mandated employment information. Designate a space on the orientation checklist that the employee can initial to confirm receipt of the materials. Providing a comprehensive orientation package can help the employee feel comfortable with the firm's infrastructure and feel cared for by the employer.

During the first week, arrange a day-by-day schedule for the new hire. Allow for at least two hours of computer training each day. Other items might include orientation meetings with office services, telecommunications, library services, marketing, and every department with whom the new employee will interact. Assign a "buddy" who can shepherd the new employee around the firm, make introductions, take the new employee to lunch on the first day, and discuss amenities available in the neighborhood, such as parking facilities, dry cleaners, and drug stores.

Computer training should be intense during the first week, with support provided on a regular basis for at least the first six months. Firms and companies that take the responsibility for actively training employees have fewer problems when it is time to upgrade systems and software. If your IT department is not large enough to maintain individual training for each employee, schedule group computer training sessions during the monthly lawyer luncheons, staff meetings, and other firm meetings that occur on a regular basis.

Companies from whom you purchase software should offer training sessions as part of the purchase price. Scheduled off-site training has the additional advantage of creating a captive audience so that lawyers are not running in and out for phone calls and secretaries are not being pulled out by lawyers for "emergencies." Training is effective only if employees make the commitment to be there and listen.

Staff Retention

Employees stay at firms for factors other than money. If employees are respected and actively listened to, if they contribute to and have a vested interest in helping the company meet its goals, they are more likely to stay with an organization. Benefits, such as flexible schedules for new parents or paternity leave, put a firm on the cutting edge of employee retention. Tuition reimbursement, sabbaticals, employer-paid dependent health coverage, and alternative work schedules are creative perks that can help retain valued employees.

9

A Blueprint for Marketing with Staff

by Robert A. Kraft

Marketing a law practice still is a tricky concept for many lawyers, full of questions that have no easy black-or-white answers. How much is too much? How slick is too slick? What about all those brochures sitting in the storeroom from our last foray into self-promotion?

My practice, a small personal injury and Social Security disability firm in Texas, eliminated a lot of the nettlesome questions that arise when setting up new ventures by deciding to put our marketing efforts into something we already had—ourselves and our staff. We do not have a separate marketing department, and I routinely remind our employees that we're all in marketing. In a small firm, everyone must contribute to the effort.

Texas has strict rules prohibiting solicitation of injury claims, so we face constraints not encountered by law firms pitching their services to corporations. Our in-house marketing efforts focus more on keeping existing clients satisfied and receiving word-of-mouth referrals than on bringing in new cases from outside sources.

We advertise on television, in the Yellow Pages and by e-mail newsletter—we even have a billboard. But no matter how much advertising we do, the bulk of our business always comes from former clients and their referrals. If you do a good job for people, they will return, and they will refer their friends to you. Naturally, you want to give them a reason to do so, and we've found our staff can be an invaluable tool in encouraging that.

Hire the Right People

Marketing with staff begins with having the right employees. For a consumer-oriented law firm, this means outgoing people with a professional attitude. Clients obviously want their lawyer and staff to be competent, but they equally want their legal team to be caring, understanding, and friendly.

A simple guideline is to hire good people, train them properly, pay them well, and keep them happy. Note that good pay doesn't necessarily guarantee happy employees. We try to show our appreciation to employees in many ways, including little perks. All employees have a business card with name and job title, and we encourage them to be liberal in handing them out. In addition to the individual cards, we keep at the front desk a stack of generic cards that have a list of practice areas printed on the back to remind visitors of the types of cases we handle.

Staff in general must be competent in their jobs, or no amount of marketing will overcome the negative impression your clients will have of your firm. Employees should be intelligent enough to make decisions on their own and motivated enough to return phone calls and e-mails promptly. If you give your employees authority to make at least some decisions, your clients will be happier because they won't have to wait as long to get answers or action. Obviously, prohibitions regarding employees giving legal advice must be heeded, but space for autonomy does exist.

Staff continuity also is an important part of marketing. We have twenty full-time employees, and half of them have worked here more than twelve years. Clients develop a great sense of confidence when they deal with the same employees throughout the course of a case, and this consideration is even more important for firms that handle long-term matters for clients rather than typically brief personal injury claims.

Opening a Case

The new client procedure in our firm begins with the receptionist. Ours is very good at fielding many calls yet still making the callers feel unhurried. She routinely keeps our client database open on her computer, which allows her to quickly look up names and direct calls to the proper employee.

For new case calls, the receptionist determines the type of case, gets a phone number in the event of an accidental disconnect, then forwards the call to an employee in the appropriate department. Every employee is authorized to take information from a new case call, so we never have to tell a caller that no one is available to talk. We try to let the callers talk for a short while before jumping in with "just the facts" questions. This lets callers know we're interested in their problems, not just in taking down the information.

If the caller's problem is obviously something we don't handle, the receptionist gives the call to a specific employee whose main job is to field such matters. This employee gets the pertinent information—we have interview sheets for various types of new case inquiries so we don't forget to ask an important question—and explains why we can't represent the caller. We average more than 40 new case calls per day. Unfortunately, about 90 percent of these are for cases we can't accept, but we still want to make a good impression on callers in the event they someday have a case we can handle.

If we don't accept a case, we make a real effort to refer the caller to a lawyer or government agency that can help. We keep a frequently updated referral list on our intranet that includes lawyers who handle cases outside our practice areas, governmental agencies, and charitable organizations. We have brochures on different legal subjects that we offer to mail; some of them are written by us and some are obtained from other sources. By spending a few minutes on the phone, providing a bit of free information, and pointing potential clients in the right direction, we let them know we do care about their problems, even if we won't be making a fee from them. This extra work takes quite a bit of staff time and may not always appear to directly benefit the firm. Some of the effort is made simply because we feel it is the right thing to do, but some clearly cultivates a potential client base.

We send a "sorry" letter to every caller we can't represent, stating we are not accepting the case and explaining any applicable statute of limitations. Again, we have form letters already drafted for various types of cases. The letter also encourages potential clients to refer friends and family to us for any legal questions and directs them to our Web site for helpful legal articles. We add all such callers to our mailing list, and we send birthday cards, calendars, and newsletters. Many clients come back to us years later, explaining that, although we couldn't help them with the original matter, they now want to hire us on a different matter. It pays to show potential clients you care about them, and it pays to keep in touch with occasional mailings.

If a new case call does sound promising, we set up an appointment at which the client meets first with a new case clerk, who enters basic information into our case management program, and then with a legal assistant, who fleshes out the details of the claim and answers most of the client's questions. The client then meets with a lawyer, who can answer any remaining questions. (All these meetings take place in a single room, with the various staff members meeting the prospective client one after another; we offer the client soft drinks and refreshments, as the visit can be lengthy.)

Immediately after opening a case, we send clients an initial letter thanking them for hiring us and reminding them of important information discussed in person. The letter also mentions that we would be happy to talk with the client's friends or family members who have unrelated legal questions, whatever they may be. I pen a short note at the bottom of each letter to personally thank the client for choosing our firm.

A few days later, we call again, thank them for hiring us, verify address and telephone information, and ask whether they forgot to tell us anything in the initial interview or have additional questions. Thirty days after signing up the case, we send another thank-you letter and a questionnaire regarding medical treatment, witnesses, and other items. We also ask whether they're satisfied with our services to date. The point of all this is to let the clients know that we really do appreciate their business and to assure them we're actively working on their cases.

Teamwork

As is obvious throughout this process, our philosophy has always been to "move work downhill" when possible. If a lawyer doesn't have to do it, let a legal assistant handle it; if the legal assistant is better used elsewhere, move the task to a legal secretary, and so on. We are scrupulous about having all work supervised by a lawyer and very careful not to let employees give legal advice or make legal decisions.

We occasionally receive client letters addressed to "Attorney Smith" although Ms. Smith is not a lawyer. We immediately send the client a letter explaining Ms. Smith's job title and stressing that she is not a lawyer. We do everything possible to avoid the trap of allowing a client to believe a staff member is a lawyer (which is one reason staff have business cards but, if not lawyers, are not listed on firm letterhead).

We take a team approach to handling files, and we encourage new clients to meet all various members of the team. This helps build rapport with the clients and eliminates the "just a voice on the line" feeling when they call us. We include photos and biographical sketches of all employees on our Web site (http://www.kraftlaw.com) and we use employees in some of our television and print advertising. The goal is to personalize the firm in the client's mind. We're proud of each of our employees, and we want our clients to know that.

Clients want lawyers and staff who communicate with them and care about their cases. In a way, our client management software allows us to show clients we care. The program we use, LawBase by Synaptec, allows us to make unlimited "activity notes" each time we take any action on a file. Whenever a client calls, the person talking with the client can see at a glance what was done on the file recently and by whom, which gives the impression that the client's file is always uppermost in our minds. (I print out all the day's activity notes and read them each evening, which lets me monitor file activity without having to pull files for a physical review.)

A vital part of showing clients you care is listening to them when they complain. But a surprising number of people don't complain when they're unhappy—they just suffer in silence and then never return or make referrals. We try to make it very easy for clients to tell us when they're not happy with our work. We keep a stack of comment cards in our waiting room, and the receptionist also hands one to each client who visits the office. The card asks simply whether the client has any comments. It may be signed or unsigned, given directly to the receptionist, or anonymously left in a box in the waiting room.

When we receive signed comment cards, we send letters thanking the client for a compliment or for pointing out a problem with our services. We call if it sounds serious. We send three questionnaires to clients during their case and each has space for comments regarding our services. We know we can answer any complaints clients may have—the trick more often is getting them actually to complain!

We try to take every opportunity to encourage existing clients to refer friends and family to us. Surprisingly, even clients who are pleased with your services may not realize they should refer their friends. Some think you're too busy to accept new clients or a small matter. Others may not realize you also handle other practice areas. Train your staff to give short cross-selling pitches to existing clients about all types of work your firm handles. (This may be especially important in a firm like ours, where some employees do nothing but Social Security work and others do nothing but personal injury work.) Make sure each employee has at least basic knowledge of the full range of services you offer.

We maintain a short list of former clients who were especially pleasant to work with or who expressed a particular interest in referring their friends. We occasionally send them postcards asking them to give us a call just so we can find out how they're doing. I created an interview form for those calls so the staff remembers to verify contact information, give news about our firm, and ask whether they have suggestions for improving our services.

The impression your staff makes is important. We can't all be young and beautiful, but we can all be clean and neatly dressed. Our firm requires a coat and tie for men and the equivalent for women, except on casual Fridays. We like the impression of professionalism this gives clients, but we do have one exception: our dress code incorporates a marketing tool—t-shirts with our firm logo on them that can be worn with casual pants on any day of the week. In addition to keeping the firm name in front of office visitors, we also get free advertising when employees go out to lunch or run errands.

Most of the "marketing" our staff does is really just being friendly, whether to potential clients, current clients, or employees at insurance companies and government agencies. We don't use high-pressure techniques and we try to keep clients from noticing that we're marketing at all. Be competent, act nice, and make sure your clients know you want more business. That's marketing in a nutshell.

Magic Numbers

We get many comments about our firm's telephone numbers: 214/999-9999 and 817/999-9999. (The first three digits are area codes for Dallas and Fort Worth, respectively.)

We got the 214 telephone number about 12 years ago when a local personal injury lawyer was closing his practice and leaving Texas. We made a deal to purchase his telephone number and his advertising space on the back cover of the Dallas Yellow Pages. (We also had to agree to take over the files he couldn't get anyone else to accept.) The 999 prefix is not in our office's geographic location, so we have to pay mileage charges each month for use of that number.

Obtaining the 817 number was a little more difficult. It was a mobile number used by the telephone company so repairpersons could check phone lines. It took quite a bit of convincing to get them to transfer the number to us. We still pay mobile phone charges for calls to that number.

We feature the phone numbers prominently in our advertising and have had many clients tell us they called because our number was easy to remember. When employees have to give their work number to a store clerk, they always get an odd look, which gives them a chance to mention our firm name.

The only real drawback to the numbers came before 10-digit dialing was required in Dallas and Fort Worth. Every day we would get dozens of calls from little kids who were just punching phone buttons. Now that everyone has to dial an area code even for local calls, that problem has disappeared.

Our Texas toll-free number is 800/989-9999. I would love to have 800/999-9999, but it's used by Covenant House, an international service agency for runaway youth. I sent a nice letter to them a few years ago and asked if they would consider selling us their telephone number. I received a rather curt reply saying my request would be passed along to Sister Mary Rose but it was doubtful she'd be interested. Apparently she wasn't, because I've heard nothing further.

Care and Feeding of the Law Office Staff 10

by Jim Calloway

The smaller the firm, the more hats the lawyer must wear. These include a dual role as management and labor, as well as chief executive officer, director of finance, director of marketing, and chief information officer. Let's discuss the lawyer as employer and as the director of human resources.

As a solo or small firm lawyer, you are an employer. (You either should be an employer or be thinking about becoming one.) The problem with many solos and small firm lawyers is that they've either never worked for someone else or they did and didn't like it. It could be that they've never really been a part of a positive employer-employee relationship, at least in their adult careers.

Some lawyers in solo practice make the decision to operate without staff. This may be done for a variety of reasons. These lawyers may be very proficient with technology and do not need secretarial assistance. They may want to have a limited or part-time practice and therefore do not want to have the overhead that comes with staff. They may have had so many bad experiences with staff that they simply don't want to spend their energy managing people, or they may simply not generate enough income to pay staff. But most lawyers find having someone to help with filing, file management, typing, telephone answering, scheduling, and a host of other tasks makes them more efficient and allows them to concentrate more on the tasks that only they can do.

In a small firm practice today, you and your employees must function as a team. This will be even more important in the future. Being a good team requires many things, but to use a clichéd sports metaphor, it generally starts with a good coach.

You want team members with skill, education, intelligence, and experience. For the small firm lawyer, attracting and keeping the best talent is a challenge. Generally speaking, a solo or small firm lawyer will not be able to compete with the largest law firms strictly on compensation for very good employees. (Luckily, those in smaller communities have a geographical advantage for the local employee.)

Assuming you want to develop excellent team members as employees, it would seem that you have two options. You can develop a system where there are clearly defined procedures and training materials. Such a system will allow replacements to easily step in when the time comes. Or you can develop a good place to work where employees feel well-treated and fairly managed. You can provide a workplace where fair rules and treatment are tempered with a bit of flexibility when it is needed to support the employee's personal and family life.

So, which office system do you want? This is obviously a trick question. The answer is: both. We'll talk about both approaches, but first let's talk about motivation.

What Motivates Employees?

A primary motivation for any of us to work is money. We work for our pay. There are very few law office employees who would not leave tomorrow if offered a chance to triple their salary. Luckily, that isn't likely to happen. The most interesting point is that surveys and studies of employees often rank compensation surprisingly low. Security, possibility of advancement, enjoyment of the type of work, and other factors often outweigh pay. Benefits also can be a motivating factor. Medical insurance is an expensive, but prized, benefit today.

Training motivates employees because people who can do their jobs more effectively are happier. Try to eliminate minor annoyances and day-to-day frustrations; even something as simple as a "cheat sheet" on keyboard shortcuts (http://jimcalloway.typepad.com/lawpracticetips/2005/02/keyboard_shortc.html) can be a helpful tool. Training can consist of bite-sized pieces like a "learn and lunch."

Threats are not an effective motivator. Fear is destructive and not a useful force over the long haul. This is a dead-end strategy. Far too many lawyers deal with their employees in the same way they deal with a recalcitrant opposing counsel or a dissembling witness. The ultimate result from this practice is that the best employees recognize that they have other options and move on, leaving you with the less capable, the easily intimidated, and those with a poor sense of self-worth.

Bonuses and profit sharing can provide motivation, but a lawyer-employer must decide on objective versus subjective criteria. Employees tend to focus on what others have received instead of what they did or didn't do. Some can see this as a system that rewards sycophancy. "If you don't do X, you won't get a bonus" transforms this from a reward to a threat. Profit sharing spawns ethical issues. Can paralegals be paid based on the profitability of the firm? The answer is a qualified yes. Law firms may give paralegals pensions, profit-sharing plans, and salary increases based on the firm's profitability. These benefits can be given based on individual performance and/or the firm's profitability. However, a firm may not base compensation on the outcome of a case. Several other jurisdictions agree with this conclusion—Philadelphia Bar Association Professional Guidance Opinion 2001-7 (2001); the Utah State Bar Ethics Advisory Opinion Committee UT Eth. Op. 02-07, 2002 WL 31079593 (Utah St. Bar); the New York State Bar Association Committee on Professional Ethics (N.Y. St. Bar Assn. Comm. Prof. Eth.); and the South Carolina Ethics Advisory Committee SC Adv. Op. 97-02, 1997 WL 582907 (S.C. Bar Eth. Adv. Comm.).

Communications Issues

Be polite and respectful to everyone. Never "chew out" an employee in front of others. If correction or negative feedback is required, do it in the privacy of your office. If the issue is of such magnitude that everyone has to be informed or reinforced about an office process, you should first talk to the offender privately and then inform him or her that you will be discussing this procedure with the rest of the employees to make sure that everyone understands. The message, "you didn't understand this and it was a problem, so I have to make sure everyone else does," is a far more positive one than, "you goofed up, and I'm going to make sure everyone knows you did."

Any major decision can be viewed as a threat if not communicated clearly. Establish official lines of communication where everyone gets announcements to prevent misunderstanding. This could be by meeting or memo or intranet. Hold regular "all-hands" meetings at least quarterly. Even if you make up your mind about a company policy matter, just say "maybe" or "probably" until you can announce it in an all-hands meeting or via the established official channel.

Job Stress

You know it. You live it. But let's all say it together: A law firm is a stressful place to work. You owe it to yourself and your staff to minimize the stress, not maximize it. It's very easy to blow up about mistakes, let off a little steam on the miscreant employee, and move on to the next projects, without realizing that you have left a large burden of hurt feelings, guilt, and anger in your wake. Reducing your employee's stress will increase retention, particularly with employees who have worked in other law offices.

Use "stress busters" to achieve a happy office. Be positive. Smile. Do something fun and unexpected for the staff at least once a year. Bring everyone together in the morning and announce that it is "Well-Tuned Machine Day" in the office and that the staff will be honored as being a well-tuned machine by demonstrating that they can finish everything they need to get done today by 3:30 p.m. so they can all leave then. End with, "and, oh, yes, everyone gets a $50 bonus today . . . well, $50 less taxes," and you will have a guaranteed success. Oklahoma City attorney Mark Robertson, 2004–2005 chair of the American Bar Association Law Practice Management Section, created the "Take Me out to the Ball Park Day." Every spring his firm closes the office for an afternoon to attend a baseball game. Have a staff luncheon where everyone is not allowed to discuss work. Celebrate birthdays. Close early on a Friday afternoon. Apologize if you lose your temper.

Differences in Age, Gender, and Culture

Avoid thinking that your way is right and others are wrong. Even if you are the sole employer, manager, hirer, and firer, you have to accept your employees for who they are. They are fallible human beings. Do some study in the area of generational differences. Accept that a 20-something's view on things will be different from those of wartime's "greatest generation." The idea of personal loyalty to an employer just because one receives a paycheck would be viewed very differently by two focus groups picked from those generations. Some people react very differently to stimuli based on their background and culture. Ethnic differences may significantly impact communications issues and reactions to being disciplined or corrected.

Hugs. I go into lots of law offices. Some of them have almost a culture of hugging. "We're like family. We hug all the time." While this may be fine with most involved, there also may be someone who is made uncomfortable by the practice. You will soon find a Generation X employee who thinks that hugging people just because you work with them is an absolutely alien concept. You might not like to hear a trial lawyer describe the office hugging policy in court should there be employer-employee litigation. Some will view this as ludicrous, but cross-gender hugging in the office should now be of the shoulder-to-shoulder "good job" type rather than the front-to-front "slow dancing" type.

Financial Reward Plans

Bonuses, profit sharing, retirement plans, longevity pay, and similar reward plans can be expensive to administer and run, but not nearly as difficult as a few years ago. Allowing only a percentage of the retirement plan to vest in the first few years should provide some incentive for employees to continue employment. Bonuses are better than raises in that they do not have to be equaled each year and worse than raises in that the employees feel that they cannot count on them. Profit-sharing plans may not work where a lawyer wants to maintain privacy about his or her income. You must decide the extent to which you are comfortable with your books—and your compensation—being open to employees. Profit-sharing plans are best when objective and based on firm financial performance that everyone understands. If you just want to award additional compensation based on profitability, attitude, and a number of other subjective factors, just call them quarterly (or semiannual) bonuses. Always keep track of the "bonus history" of each employee—you may not recall the past exactly, but they will.

If you decide to have a profit-sharing plan, it will focus everyone on the firm's profitability, both for better and for worse. You may have to defend that three-day business trip to Las Vegas for a CLE program.

Office Policies and Procedures Manual

Even though many small firm lawyers may dislike the idea of documenting office policies in writing, it is a critical part of the "fairness" equation. The twenty-first-century lawyer cannot afford to act as if no disgruntled employee could ever successfully sue a lawyer-employer. It happens frequently these days.

Draft a hypothetical 15- or 20-year calendar and see what incentives will be there through that time period. For example, your paid-leave policy may increase when an employee has been with you five or 10 consecutive years. One may vest fully in the retirement plan after four years. A 20-year employee may have voluntary retirement contributions matched two-to-one instead of one-to-one up to a certain limit. If there are years when there are no incentive events, just make some up. One example might be the "Lucky Seven"—an employee who completes seven consecutive years' employment with the firm shall be granted an additional two weeks' pay to be paid in the next regular pay period after the anniversary date of hire.

In a similar vein, you should keep a personnel file for each employee and make entries in it, both positive and negative, as circumstances warrant. Always provide a copy of such entries to the employee with a written notice that he or she has 10 days to provide a written response or explanation, which will also be a part of the file.

Obviously, paying employees for overtime work will be both fair and popular. It may also be expensive. However, with the passage of recent federal legislation, it also may no longer be as ambiguous a situation as it was in the past. (For more information on overtime pay, see the article "The Lawyer as Employer: Why Do They Keep Changing the Rules?" (Vol 24., No. 1, *GP|Solo Magazine*, January/February 2007, http://www.abanet.org/genpractice/magazine/2007/jan-feb/lawyerasemployer.html).

The Bottom Line

Be a nice boss and a fair employer, attempting always to treat others with respect and being quick to apologize and make amends when you fail. Go out of your way to maintain a safe, positive, professional, and nonthreatening workplace. Listen carefully to your employees' requests for workplace improvements and err on the side of granting them when you can (e.g., providing a bottled-water dispenser even though the tap water doesn't taste that bad to you). Pay special attention to office ergonomics and the possibility of repetitive stress injuries. You want to avoid both employees trying to work in pain as well as workers' compensation claims.

Be aware of the fact that law offices tend to be stressful places to work. Do your part to avoid unnecessary stress, both by your attitude and your actions. You may be unconcerned about starting the final proofing of a brief in the afternoon on the day it is due—some lawyers actually get a little adrenaline charge out of this—but it will drive your staff nuts, particularly those organized and efficient types we like to see in our law offices.

Handle employment matters in writing, starting with the letter that new hires receive on their first day congratulating them and outlining their pay and their benefits with references to the office policy manual (and their "at will" status if applicable). The lawyer who has no written office policies manual or employee's manual has a fool for a human resources director.

You may think preparation of an office procedures manual is a waste of time, but you won't think so when a valued employee is suddenly gone. Investing a few hours each month in developing this resource can lead to significant gains in efficiency. It will also make it easier to safely delegate tasks to less-skilled junior staff. If employees tell you that they think you are preparing this so you can easily replace them, tell the employees candidly that you don't want to lose them but want to be prepared if you do.

Conduct regular reviews of each staff person. Discuss shortcomings and successes. This is very difficult but is a key to the employee's believing that the workplace is fair. It is a cliché but nevertheless true that employees do what you inspect rather than what you expect. It should be known within the office that raises are considered on an employee's anniversary date of hire or some common calendar date. In the same way, it should be known in the office when bonuses may occur. Mid-December annual bonuses are traditional and benefit employees with extra holiday expenses. You may decide on a quarterly or semiannual schedule. One exception to this rule is a large financial windfall to the firm. When this is collected, it is generally good to "share the wealth" at the next pay period with a bonus while everyone is excited about the good fortune.

Meet with a financial adviser about setting up a 401(k) or other firm retirement plan. Set reasonable vesting requirements and make it easy for a departing employee to transfer the balance to another entity for management. With all of the recent talk about Social Security and retirement, it is increasingly less likely that you will be able to maintain qualified employees with no retirement plan no matter how good the compensation you pay. The American Bar Association Members Retirement Program offers plans appropriate for the small firm, and ABA membership is not required (http://www.abaretirement.com).

Have a family-friendly workplace. Recognize that, for most employees, their job is only a means to an end and their family is of primary importance. Be as flexible as you can, understanding that other employees may attempt to take advantage for themselves if you are too generous with one.

Maslow's Hierarchy and Employee Motivation

Most of you have heard of Abraham H. Maslow, who developed the "Hierarchy of Needs" model in the 1940s and 1950s. His theory is that we must satisfy each level of need before moving on to satisfy the next one:

1. Biological and physical needs (air, food, drink, shelter, warmth, sex, sleep, etc.).
2. Safety needs (protection from the elements, security, order, law, stability).
3. Belongingness and love needs (co-workers, family, affection, relationships, etc.).
4. Esteem needs (self-esteem, achievement, mastery, independence, status, dominance, prestige, managerial responsibility).
5. Self-actualization needs (realizing personal potential, self-fulfillment, seeking personal growth and peak experiences).

Others have added and modified Maslow's work to reflect their opinion of our changing times:

6. Cognitive needs (knowledge, meaning).
7. Aesthetic needs (appreciation and search for beauty, balance, form).
8. Transcendence needs (helping others to achieve self-actualization).

This hierarchy is easily applicable to employee motivation. If your employee feels in physical danger because your office is located in a crime-ridden part of town, it is doubtful that any incentive package will persuade that employee to continue in your employ for long. (For more about Maslow, see http://www.businessballs.com/maslow.htm.)

11 Keys to Success: Leadership, Attorney-Staff Relations, and Simplified Action Planning

by Nancy Byerly Jones

Are employee bickering, low morale, and/or low productivity dragging down your office? Are you tired of failing to accomplish your goals year after year? Do you feel you could be a more effective leader? Would you like someone like yourself to be your supervisor? In short, are you in control of your work, or is it in control of you? Talk is cheap—it's easy to sound good discussing our desires to be excellent leaders, the benefits of organization and efficiency, our pride in timely and excellent work product, and other lofty goals we'd like to achieve.

However, turning our "talk" into actions and our good intentions into positive, productive steps is much easier said than done in our 90-mile-per-hour lives. Just surviving yet another chaotic day is a worthy accomplishment itself in today's ever-changing legal system. Unfortunately, living in survival mode means that many—if not most—of our goals will remain just that: mere aspirations instead of solid achievements. As a result, our stress levels soar while our morale and our productivity spiral downward.

This chapter offers an overview of three areas—leadership, attorney/staff relations, and simplified action planning—that usually need significant attention in offices where goals remain unattained year after year, risk management flounders, stress soars way too high, and morale plummets.

Leadership

We are all leaders, whether by formal title (e.g., managing partner) or by actions such as supervising and training associates and support staff, setting a good example, handling conflict, etc. Unfortunately, some people lead in name only. They like the title but do not manage the responsibilities a true leader must bear. Sometimes it's just easier to put our heads in the sand than it is to face the anguish and exhaustion of making tough decisions (whether to terminate an unsatisfactory employee, for example). The cost of not facing responsibility is high and includes lower productivity, increased malpractice risks, and poor office morale.

Leaders and managers. Leadership and management differ from each other. A manager oversees and handles day-to-day issues that must be addressed in order to carry out the firm's objectives: personnel management, filing financial reports, handling computer and other technology requirements, ordering office supplies, etc. A leader plays the role of visionary, planner, motivator, negotiator, and final decision maker for an office. Leaders are responsible for creating short- and long-term action plans for the firm, developing constructive and realistic marketing plans, and delegating as appropriate. If they try to take on the manager's role as well, they risk not having the time or energy to be effective.

Changing times. It wasn't that long ago that one of the biggest challenges facing firm leaders was how to divide the pie fairly. We now have a greater diversity within the profession than ever before. Female law school graduates outnumber male graduates for the first time in history, and the profession reflects the multicultural and multiracial makeup of our population. Lawyers in active practice range from newcomers in their mid-20s to old-school traditionalists in their

80s, and they may work in a solo practice with one assistant or be one of more than 1,000 lawyers at a sprawling mega-firm. The age and wage gaps can sometimes produce misunderstandings and tensions.

Other high-pressure issues that lawyers did not face in the past may include the following: more competition, both externally and internally; marketing and rainmaking pressures; realities of today's buyer's market; client expectations and demands for immediate turnaround; decreased loyalty of employers to employees, and vice versa; and media-influenced "me-only" attitudes instead of team spirit and collegiality.

Look in the mirror. We all think we know how others could improve their personal interactions, communication, and leadership skills. But it is a good idea to stop the world long enough (at least once a year, preferably more often) to conduct self-audits regarding our own skills. Questions you might ask yourself in order to decide what you can keep on doing and what you should change include:

- Do I have a realistic long-term plan for my firm, and has it been communicated clearly to all employees?
- Do I set examples with my habits and behavior that are consistent with what I demand from others?
- Am I keeping my employees motivated?
- Do I adapt well to change, or do I cling hopelessly to worn-out systems and traditions?
  How would my peers, staff, and clients describe me as a leader?
- When I leave the firm, will I leave a realistic and attainable plan for future growth and prosperity?

Motivation. Being truly happy with what you do will radiate and affect all those with whom you work. If you are fighting burnout, unsatisfied with the practice of law, and more frustrated than not with most of your clients, this, too, will be felt by your peers and staff—and such feelings can be highly contagious. Motivating others is not difficult, as long as we have a good assessment of the pros and cons of our own work and the positives outweigh the negatives. If this is not the case, motivating others is next to impossible because our actions speak so much louder than our words.

Another factor that can influence morale is inconsistent management. Make sure you have clear rules and procedures within your office that are enforced consistently and fairly. Nothing lowers morale quicker than different rules and privileges for certain employees (such as arriving and leaving at specific times). Preferential treatment does not sit well with those who make the effort (or, in many cases, special arrangements for child care) to be on time.

There's an old saying, "When I'm right, who remembers, and when I'm wrong, who forgets!" When constructive criticism is needed, discuss the issue in private. Conversely, be public with praise. A simple "thank you, great job" goes a long, long way.

Strive to be aware of and resolve underlying tensions among the partners or shareholders. Lawyers often say they have an unresolved "issue" with a partner or associate but no one else in the office is aware of it. Not so! Others may not know the details of the dispute, but they indeed sense and suffer from the tensions emitted by feuding colleagues. We humans always will have our differences and opinions, but we can learn how to deal with disputes quickly and in a spirit of compromise. Putting our heads in the sand only aggravates the problem and sends the message that childish and destructive grudges are acceptable.

Self-care. Perhaps the most important and most often ignored adage in the legal profession is "Take care of yourself!" We all know that without our good health nothing else matters, so why do lawyers so consistently put ourselves last when it comes to healthy diets, time off, and exercise? It just makes sense—physical and financial—to take good care of ourselves and encourage coworkers to do the same. Yet some folks never take a break from the office and, worse, try to make colleagues feel guilty for taking sick or vacation time. Lawyers who act that way hurt themselves as well as their firms; the best employees are those who maintain a healthy balance between their personal and professional lives.

Attorney/Staff Relations

The lawyer's role. Lawyers often are stunned to receive a highly valued employee's unexpected resignation, but, in many cases, the departing staff member sent out numerous warning signals. They requested more time off, were irritable, and showed signs of exhaustion from the demanding and overwhelming workload; but the responsible attorneys did not take the signs of burnout seriously enough. The risk of such surprises, however, is significantly reduced when lawyers promote open and constructive communication with staff members and treat each employee as a valued and respected member of the office. Similarly, staff members help ensure better attorney/staff relations when they disclose and handle problems quickly and professionally rather than gossiping behind the parties' backs. Good team players work with the firm's best interests at heart.

The list below offers guidelines for lawyers who want to establish and maintain good working relationships with support staff. Use it to review strengths and weaknesses of attorney/staff relations within your firm.

The lawyer's duty to instruct and guide staff is ongoing. You may do the teaching yourself or delegate this task to an experienced trainer. When new employees start, and periodically thereafter, set aside time for them to learn and periodically review the following essentials.

- The ins and outs of their job responsibilities and duties. Create written job descriptions and give one to every employee; revise them on a timely basis when duties change.
- The Rules of Professional Conduct. Each employee should read the Rules and have opportunities to ask questions about them.
- The ability to distinguish what constitutes "offering legal advice," which, of course, only a lawyer is permitted to do. Staff can explain legal processes to clients but cannot advise clients about rights and duties in relation to another, represent clients in court, or select the legal documents that are appropriate for a client's legal situation.
- Office and risk management policies and systems. These may include docket/calendaring control, checking for conflicts of interest, file management, firm security, documentation essentials, proper use of checklists, current software programs, telephone procedures, etc.
- Confidentiality. You cannot stress to often that all client matters must be strictly confidential, both within and outside the office. Employees should sign a firm confidentiality form that docu-

ments confidentiality standards and procedures and clearly states that a breach of confidentiality may result in immediate dismissal.
- The importance of excellent client relations. Be sure you set a continuous good example by returning telephone calls promptly, keeping clients regularly informed, being on time for appointments, etc.

Additional ways to establish and maintain good working relationships with support staff include the following:

- Regularly provide assistants with feedback regarding the quality of their work through scheduled staff meetings and work evaluation sessions.
- Encourage membership in legal assistant associations.
- Offer financial assistance for continuing education opportunities.
- Include books and articles on ethics, malpractice prevention, and relevant areas of law within your firm's library, and encourage staff to read them.
- Provide a positive work environment. Keep in mind the responsibilities and pressures that accompany staff work.
- Avoid too-busy-for-you, better-than-you, and similarly arrogant attitudes that promote low office morale, disloyalty, and costly mistakes.
- Have and share a good sense of humor!
- Be alert for signs of staff disgruntlement, conflicts, or other problems. Provide procedures for anonymously reporting suspected substance abuse, ethical violations, or mental health crises.
- Respect your staff, and thank them often for their contributions to jobs well done.

The staff's role. Office staff play many integral roles within a law practice. They assist with administrative and clerical tasks, marketing, good client relations, avoiding malpractice, handling client complaints, and potential conflicts of interest. A lawyer's success can be highly dependent on the ways staff function, doing their part to promote a positive working environment. On a personal or firm-wide level, success goals can be incorporated into daily routines:

- Seek out and welcome educational opportunities.
- Share personal knowledge and experiences that can benefit the office.
- Empathize with supervisors' and coworkers' pressures from and responsibilities to clients, the office, and the legal system.
- Avoid office gossip like the plague.
- In addition to raising matters of concern, propose possible solutions.
- Join legal associations.
- Know the firm's risk-management policies and systems, understand them, respect them, use them, and offer suggestions for improvement.
- Avoid "I'm just here for the paycheck" and other unprofessional attitudes.
- Maintain a good sense of humor and a positive attitude. Balancing professional and personal commitments equally helps.
- Express your respect for and appreciation of coworkers' assistance, guidance, and support, and acknowledge their successes.

Everyone's Responsibility

Although successful attorney/staff relations depend on many factors, these can be summed up in just a few words: mutual respect and effective communication. If attorneys and staff have genuine respect for one another and communicate clearly and effectively, most of the other essential elements of good employer/employee relations fall naturally into place. Conducting regular self-audits helps everyone stay in touch with how they are doing, whether managers, leaders, or support staff.

Each person within a law firm, whether practicing law or sorting the mail, is responsible for building and maintaining healthy, respectful, and productive relationships. When office leaders don't set a good example, the ripple effect within the office can be devastating. When everyone takes this responsibility to heart and puts it into actual practice, however, a win-win situation for everyone results.

Simplified Strategic Planning and Goal Setting

More often than not, our list of desired objectives remains just that—possibilities rather than accomplishments. Our intentions may be good and determined, but life has a way of hitting us with so many unforeseen events that it seems we struggle just to put out the resultant fires. This leaves most people with little time for reaching their preferred objectives.

Based on my experience as a law office manager, a practicing attorney, and now a legal management consultant, I believe three things are critical to increase the odds of reaching our goals:

1. Make a written list of objectives.
2. Map step by step what needs to be done, by whom, and when.
3. Monitor your progress and hold yourself and others accountable to your commitments.

Keeping this formula simple works best. Although some firms pay a lot of money to have complex and voluminous strategic plans prepared, most of those plans go unread. Our good intentions to plow through the material somehow never seem to translate into action. On the other hand, when strategic plans are written in a simpler and shorter manner (I call these "action plans"), office leaders are much more apt to review and assist in monitoring them. A sample of one possible simplistic format is included in the appendix of my book, *Easy Self Audits for the Busy Law Office* (ABA 1999).

In my experience, building a successful law practice takes courage, foresight, an open mind, and time to come to full fruition. Fortunately, however, with a heavy dose of patience and determination, you can indeed make many positive changes for your office, your clients, and yourself. Best of all, the changes last, which surely beats living with the constant chaos and stress of a disorganized, poorly managed office that seems to survive only on a day-by-day basis.

12 Motivating Lawyers and Employees in the Small Law Office

by Jim Karger

"WORK sucks!"

We've all heard that before. Most have said it. Today, more than half of all employees in the United States do not find their jobs even "reasonably satisfying." So, if you didn't get up this morning rearing to get to work, it may be sad, but it is normal.

Happiness, satisfaction, and contentment with work have been falling for years. The Conference Board, a highly regarded business research organization, regularly surveys Americans on how satisfied they are with their lives, including their work lives. In 1995 their survey indicated that 59 percent of workers were "reasonably satisfied" with their jobs. Not ecstatic, not happy, not content, but "reasonably satisfied."

By 2000, the number of employees "reasonably satisfied" with their jobs plunged to 51 percent. In 2003 the number fell to less than half, the lowest percentage of satisfied employees since the Conference Board began its survey. Even among workers who enjoy the largest paychecks, contentment with work fell more than 10 percent in less than a decade.

So unsatisfying is work for most employees today that fully half say they would choose a lower-paying job they like over a higher-paying job they hate, yet few make that leap. Why? Because most employees have far too much stuff they have bought but not paid for. Others want more stuff. Others are simply trying to survive. Regardless of reason, most employees start each morning the same way—hit the "snooze" button on the alarm clock at least three times, get up, trudge to the job, find little or no satisfaction or happiness there, smile when the boss is looking, grit their teeth when he's not, collect their paycheck on Friday, and repeat the cycle until retirement, burn out, or death— whichever comes first.

Why? Here are some common responses:

- I decided what I was going to do when I was young, before I really knew what work was all about.
- I never discovered my passion in life. I went to work instead.
- I know what I'd like to do, but I don't think I could make a living doing it.
- I liked my job in the beginning, but over the years I've gotten tired of it.
- My work has changed.
- My boss has changed.
- I've changed. What was important to me at 21 isn't what is important to me at 50.
- I'm good at what I do. I don't know how to do anything else.

And, to some degree, many employees don't get much satisfaction from their jobs because their jobs were designed to maximize efficiency and productivity, not to satisfy the incumbent or make them happy.

Nowhere do these observations seem truer than in a law office, yet we know that to hire and retain the best lawyers and staff, they need to be motivated. They need to like their jobs.

In this chapter we briefly look at areas in which the partners/shareholders in small law firms need to keep in mind and embrace if motivation of lawyers and staff is a goal.

Compensation

Surveys regularly find lawyers near the top of highly compensated professions. Indeed, the average lawyer today makes $100,000 a year. Yet, practicing law does not make the top 10 in many surveys of "best" professions. Paralegals and administrative personnel even have it worse—all the pressure without the money.

Indeed, some consider law to be one of the world's worst professions. Ben Mathis-Lilley, observing these results, concludes, "Don't go to law school. Lawyers are 3.6 times more likely to be depressed than members of other professions, and it's not just because their jobs are more stressful. For most people, job stress has little effect on happiness unless it is accompanied by a lack of control (lawyers, of course, have clients to listen to) or involves taking something away from somebody else (a common feature of the legal system)."

Yet, many young law graduates are attracted to the law because it pays more than some of the other vocations they evaluated. It is not surprising. The biggest law firms are paying top graduates up to $180,000 a year to start and twice that by the time they make partner.

Compensation like that makes it tough for smaller firms to compete for top talent. Yet, for most small law firms the hiring and retaining of employees is relegated to a singular dimension—economics. Most employers believe, even if they say they don't, that as long as they pay a competitive wage and offer a nice basket of traditional benefits they can and will attract and retain top talent.

Like most axioms that are not true, there is a modicum of truth to the premise that money is the answer. It is true that if you don't pay competitively, no one, lawyer, paralegal, or administrator, is coming to work for you and if they do come to work for you they will only stay as long as it takes to be offered a position with a firm that does pay competitively.

Note I said "competitively," not fairly. Note I did not say they leave because they are "not paid enough." Few people believe they are paid "enough" and most employees don't believe they are paid what they are worth. But because most employees understand that labor is a commodity, most employees don't fret over the fact they're not paid "enough" as long as they make as much as the guy in the next office or down the street doing the same or similar job.

An example outside the law: The employee flipping burgers at McDonald's knows he makes only a fifth as much as a tool and die maker across the street at Boeing, and that doesn't bother him just as long as the fry-cook next door at Burger King isn't taking home more than he does.

The same is true inside the law. Most small law firms have lost valuable associates and support personnel because they lost connection with what the market requires to retain talent.

The bottom line is money is an answer, but it is not an answer to the question, "What makes employees happy and satisfied in the long term?" Rather, money is the answer to the question, "What demotivates employees if it is not competitive?" Another way of saying is that money is not a long-term motivator. Rather, it is more often a long-term demotivator to any employee not paid competitively.

A way to think about wages and traditional benefits is that they are the ante into the card game. You don't win by throwing in your ante, but you can't play the game if you don't ante up.

That is why I remain puzzled at the number of employers, including law firms, who fail to perform detailed and regular pay and benefits studies, who don't conduct or participate in local wage and benefits surveys, but rather use guesswork to establish their pay and benefits plans. By not knowing the competitive landscape in any geographic area for labor, whether it be for a business-generating partner or a receptionist, one is destined to make mistakes, either on the high or low side, and these are the employers who end up trading employees back and forth, in great part because their wages and benefits don't reflect the market, internally or externally.

That said, there are temporal anomalies, periods of time when employees will stay and will perform if only because they are in a poor economy and fear layoff and the inability to get an equivalent job. The first two or three years of a young lawyer's career are a good example. Most are not worth very much until they have had some on-the-job training and practical experience. But, once they have obtained that training and experience, they become more marketable and this leads to the common complaint of small firm partners: "We train them and then another firm comes and takes them away." Nice try, but not true. The other firm didn't take them away. They left because their firm failed to know and adjust wages and traditional benefits to take into account their employees' skill and experience

Career Path

A second *faux pas* endemic to the American workplace, including law firms, especially small law firms, is employee dissatisfaction associated with a lack of career path—no mobility upward, or at least no arrow pointing the way to the top.

This is not to say every young lawyer wants to be a partner, but many, perhaps most, do. Some can and will move up the organization if they are shown exactly what will be required over what period of time in order to become a partner/shareholder and what it means to be a partner/shareholder in your law firm. If you don't give young lawyers a path, they will eventually leave to find an employer who will.

Management Skills

Ironically, most lawyers are destined to be managers, yet in law school they receive no training on how to manage others. Every lawyer-manager should remember the following when dealing with employees:

- Communicate expectations clearly. Too many lawyers speak in legal shorthand and perceive themselves too busy to communicate their expectations in detail; yet detail is what they want in their product.
- Don't prejudge. Every employee has something unique to offer your firm, and it is your job to discover it and work it into your vision for your firm.
- Ensure that every employee has the tools to do is or her job well. A common complaint among young lawyers in smaller firms is that they are at a disadvantage to their big firm counterparts because they do not have the resources. Whether it is technology, library, online services, or some other tool necessary to do their job effectively and efficiently, it is important that they have it to eliminate this common area of dissatisfaction.
- Know your employees. Know what motivates each one of them and learn what it takes to mentor each of them to become the best they can be.
- Encourage employees to spend time on continuing education, and not just for the lawyers. Make sure everyone is involved in staying "cutting edge" in his or her fields of expertise.

- Evaluate your employees' performance and have them evaluate yours. Too few small law firms have a formal performance evaluation procedure. Bottom line? It is difficult to know how you are performing if no one in the know tells you. Likewise, if one of your goals is to improve as a manager, it behooves you to ask those you manage how you are doing in an atmosphere where they know there will be no retaliation for a poor review.
- Recognize employees for excellent performance in meaningful ways. Whether it is a dinner for two for an associate and spouse or a week's trip to Mexico for your "employee of the year," know that while you may not get what you want, you will always get what you reward. By the same token, do not tolerate substandard performance; coach and train and if that doesn't work, remove.
- Actively listen. When an employee is in your office, turn off the phone, put your Blackberry in your desk or turn it off, and ask your secretary not to interrupt. Then listen actively, not passively, to the employee. You will make better decisions and they will know and appreciate your effort.
- Be transparent. Share information openly, accurately, and timely. Only then do employees feel engaged and involved.
- Consistency pays. Many lawyers, under pressures of a practice, can be inconsistent in handling people. The level manager is the best manager. They treat the janitor in the same way they treat a client or partner.
- Celebrate successes. There are no individual successes, only those of your firm. When milestones are reached, celebrate them and involve everyone.

Beyond the Dollar—Credible Connections

A good management style and competitive pay and benefits alone are not enough to engender long-term employee satisfaction. What can the smaller law firm do to retain its employees and get the discretionary effort from everyone in the office necessary to be competitive in an ever more competitive industry? The answer is to connect to employees at a different level, more like we connect to our families and friends, and, most important, this is where the small firm has an advantage—if they but use it.

What this requires is a new paradigm for some, one that recognizes that our employees are not just human resources, but human beings, too. We need to connect *to* our employees *through* those connections most important to them.

Beyond regular and transparent communications that lead employees to conclude they are in on things, there are "credible connections" —the people and life dynamics that mean the most to us and the opportunity to make them a part of the work experience for every employee, to include:

- family,
- friends,
- work involvement,
- civic involvement,
- charitable service, and
- institutional connections

On an institutional level, there are many ways to connect to our employees. Employee participation teams, for example, recognize the human need for interdependence and the need to know we make a difference. It acts to dispel the commonly held belief that somehow we should be independent, that we pull our own strings, that we are individually responsible for our own successes, rather than the more real, but less ego-based understanding that most of our success comes from being in the right place at the right time with the right people, that we all get weak from time to time and need others to help us paddle the canoe. This means involving others in your firm in projects to enhance productivity, rather than assuming that the partners always know best.

Other examples of institutional opportunities to make credible connections include:

- *Civic involvement.* Some employees are connected to their communities. Encouraging and supporting their involvement in community activities enhances their connection with your firm.
- *Charitable service.* Human empathy cannot be overestimated. Some of the nation's best companies encourage charitable involvement and, indeed, provide time off with pay to employees to serve a charity of their choice. Whether it is making some

soup for a homeless person, collecting clothes for a shelter, taking food cans to a food bank, or providing services to a animal humane society, there are myriad ways our employees can and want to serve. There are few credible connections more powerful than seeing one's employer as humane.

- *Environmental activities.* Connecting with employees through their connection with our earth reminds us all of our obligation to leave it better than we found it. The 20-something generation is serious about the environment and its members are exhibiting social responsibility and concerns that earlier generations did not. Green is here and it is here to stay. If you don't get on the bandwagon, a lot of the best and brightest will pass you by.
- *Financial education.* Debt and credit, financial planning, monthly budgets, and living trusts are all part of a financial education that many employees, including those in law firms, never received. Providing opportunities to learn more about money and how to handle it effectively is still another credible connection that can be provided at a low cost.
- *Reward and recognition programs.* Employees cannot be praised too often for service to your firm. Whether it be for quality service, attendance, volunteerism, or any other positive contribution by an employee, this credible connection recognizes the truth that you don't get what you want, but rather you get what you reward.
- *Breaking bread.* It's hard to intensely dislike someone you have broken bread with. Whether it is a BBQ for employees and their families or lunch with your firm's top partners once a year, each is a credible connection.

Get creative. In the *New York Times* article, "For Lawyers, Perks to Fit a Lifestyle," Lynnley Browning cites some of the creative perks provided by firms of various sizes, including:

- a "happiness committee" charged with performing random acts of kindness, such as leaving small gifts on the desks of lawyers, paralegals, and assistants;
- theatre and sports tickets, dry cleaning services, even taking an employee's car to the repair shop in recognition of the hours worked;

- down payments on hybrid cars;
- Personal coaching to deal with the all too common stress, anxiety, and depression found in law offices;
- yoga classes; and
- power nap rooms.

Connections One on One

As powerful as they are, institutional connections alone won't bring the small law firm to the post-modern workplace, one in which there is no longer two lives—the "work life" and the "real life"—but the reality of one life, with one fitting into the other seamlessly and working together to make a better life.

The foundation for an employer, any employer, is the relationship between each employee and his or her manager. In the end, they are "the company" to most employees. More companies recognize this and understand the value of managers really knowing their employees—what they value, their spouse, their children, their personal interests, and all that is important to them.

While you cannot teach someone who doesn't care to care, you can provide someone who does care with the tools to show it and, in the end, even those who don't care can learn to care by changing their behavior. Caring and compassionate supervisors and managers remember the important things, such as the names of employees' children, and acknowledges births, deaths, illnesses, anniversaries, weddings, and personal interests. It takes a system to do it right, but such connections, which are often pushed under the rug or sublimated to economics, are finally being recognized for what they are worth—everything. In the end, work is a form of relationship. It can be one that is limited to a trade of money for services or it can be more, one filled with care and compassion.

Indeed, executives of *Fortune* 1,000 companies surveyed by Cornell University's Johnson Graduate School of Management recently were asked, "What is the most important characteristic of tomorrow's business leader?" Their answer, "Compassion will be one of the most important characteristics business leaders will need for success a decade from now." Indeed, only "team building" was cited more often than compassion by the executives, who selected from a list that also included the terms "competitiveness," "intelligence," and "aggressiveness."

The majority (58 percent) of these executives strongly agreed that businesses have a responsibility to address social issues and become more involved with family, diversity, equal rights, and the environment, yet only 14 percent strongly agreed that corporate leaders are doing a good job addressing those issues.

Conclusion

William Wordsworth said it best: "The best portion of a good man's life are his little, nameless, unremembered acts of kindness." It is the challenge of some of America's most vibrant and profitable small law firms to determine how best to manifest this simple truth in our workplaces.

Part IV

Paralegal and Legal Assistants

Traditionally, receptionists (who frequently doubled as secretaries) were the only office personnel who had direct contact with clients. Others toiled away deep in the recesses of the office. Now, paralegals and legal assistants often have direct contact with clients, clients' employees, judges, opposing counsel, and witnesses, performing a wide variety of tasks to ease lawyers' burdens and enhance their productivity. The face and alter ego of a law practice has become more than simply the person manning the front desk.

13 Paralegals—You've Come a Long Way

by William I. Weston

The practice of law, especially by solo and small firm practitioners has changed dramatically over the past 30 years. Before then, the practice revolved around the lawyer personally. All decisions, all control, all systems revolved around the lawyer as an individual. Often the lawyer was assisted by a secretary and sometimes by a law clerk. Those support individuals were there to do the bidding of the lawyer. As time passed, the law clerk left the firm to finish law school and was replaced by a string of law clerks, each leaving after a relatively short period of time. But the secretary remained and became more adept at a variety of tasks. These tasks included the usual secretarial work as well as managing the escrow and office accounts, talking with clients when the lawyer was not available, and, at times, completing basic forms as they became more routine. The role of the secretary increased in competence but not as a professional.

As recognition of those skills and the loyalty that came with them, the lawyer would reward the secretary by creating the position known as "legal secretary." In those early days, the position did not have specific duties but rather was the product of longevity and experience. At the same time, a number of programs evolved to teach people how to provide paraprofessional services in a legal setting. The job was called paralegal or legal assistant. No one really knew what the position meant. There was, in those early days, recognition that some of the functions of the law firm could be effectively performed by individuals who were properly trained in a manner more formal and more professional than through the experience gained through longevity in a law office. That is not to suggest that the law firm-trained secretary was ineffective, but the training came from experiences within that law firm and were based on techniques used by that law firm. What was missing was the exposure to a variety of learning experiences that came from a more formal education.

Many of the early paralegal programs were certificate programs, which provided a credential after a relatively short grouping of courses. Legal secretary certificate programs also developed and, for the first time, employees in a law firm other than the lawyer were afforded a limited type of professional position instead of a position that resulted from longevity. As the certificate programs became more successful, community colleges and then four-year colleges developed more formalized paralegal programs leading first to an associate's degree and then ultimately to a bachelor's degree.

For the first time, there was a new class of professionals available to lawyers—people with formal training in areas such as civil litigation, torts and contracts, criminal law, and legal research. Instead of the individual trained on the job, the lawyer could select a professional who could perform tasks that would allow the lawyer to engage in activities that maximized the lawyer's training, background, and experience. Yet, the use of paralegals has been slow, and among those most reluctant to take this step are the solo and small firm practitioners.

Among the major reasons suggested for this reluctance, two are most common—economics and trust. The economics of paralegal utilization are important to understand. There is concern among solo and small firm practitioners that utilization of a paralegal will result in increased cost to the firm. The reality is the exact opposite. Utilizing a paralegal to do those tasks for which the paralegal is properly trained will allow the lawyer to bring in more business and to perform the work of the case more efficiently and more economically by spreading the responsibilities out among staff members whose hourly costs are much lower than that of the lawyer. The paralegal can multi-task on a variety of case matters while the lawyer focuses on client issues, trial work, and new business. This approach also puts the lawyer in the position of supervising the work of others rather than having to do the work.

In addition, the paralegal can assume other duties in the office and remove the responsibility from the lawyer, again freeing the lawyer to bring in new business and engage in those tasks only an lawyer can do. Among these paralegal tasks are office management and, especially, technology management. As the practice of law becomes more technology-oriented, with electronic filing and electronic discovery, the need for a competent professional who understands hardware and software and the protocols associated with both becomes even greater.

Although it is common for lawyers to believe that they can do everything, it is impossible for the lawyer to be competent in technology, practice management, and human resources, and still function effectively as a lawyer. Every lawyer today has to have some fundamental computer knowledge to supervise the operation of the office and to be able to handle the tremendous amount of records and documents associated with client representation. Some lawyers have more than fundamental knowledge. But they cannot develop the expertise and devote the attention needed to sustain technological competence. In addition, the legal world today demands great speed and accuracy in documents and, therefore, the use of technology to accomplish those goals. Finally, the effective use of technology reduces the costs of the delivery of legal services and increases the ability of the practitioner to provide safeguards as to quality of services.

The properly trained paralegal is an indispensible employee in managing technology. This includes the determination of technology needs both for hardware and software; the training of individuals in the law firm on the use of the equipment and software; the establishment and maintenance of firm records and information management; and interfacing with technology professionals. Paralegals who graduate today from quality programs have been exposed to both hardware and software and have hands-on experience with both. Paralegals who graduate from quality programs have very often taken law office management courses and technology courses that allow them to understand the latest in technology management issues. This allows the paralegal to bring the skills of law office management together with an understanding of the legal system and the requirements of the delivery of legal services in a law firm setting. For the busy solo or small form practitioner, the availability of such skills adds an enormous level of competence to the firm and helps to guarantee success for the practitioner. Having a paralegal allows the practitioner to focus on the quality of the legal services, the quality of client services, and contact and the important acquisition of a steady stream of new business, instead of attending to a panorama of management issues.

The second area of expressed concern regarding paralegals is trust. The one aspect of solo or small firm practice that is attractive to the lawyer is absolute control over all aspects of the practice and of the lawyer's life. While there may be pressures from the courts and from clients, the lawyer alone makes the decisions as to how those pressures are manifest and how every detail of every case and every issue will be handled. No matter escapes the control of the lawyer or, for that matter, the responsibility. Many lawyers fear that, by having a paralegal, they will have the responsibility without the control. Having total control is a very satisfying aspect of law practice because the practitioner knows or hopes that he or she can minimize risks by maintaining control. Those tasks that are parceled out to a secretary or to a law clerk can remain under the strict control of the lawyer and the ultimate decisions as to the management of the office, technology, purchasing, and the escrow account, among other things, must bear the control and the satisfaction of the lawyer.

In that type of situation, to allow a professional (other than another lawyer) to have some area of control is, at minimum, concerning. Suddenly there is another person who is indeed an employee; but is professionally trained and will expect to be able to make some decisions independently and to take responsibilities for some aspects of the operation of the law practice. In addition, the lawyer is ethically responsible and legally responsible for this new professional—the paralegal—so that the lawyer must also take time from the practice and management of the firm to engage in training. The combination of "letting go" and training presents a daunting obstacle for some solo and small firm practitioners. There is some basis for the concern. The paralegal can make a mistake or take on a responsibility that may be inappropriate. This could lead to liability for the lawyer or even a visit from the bar counsel. The paralegal could provide the client with information that exceeds the role of the paralegal resulting in unauthorized practice of law by the paralegal and at least embarrassment for the firm. The paralegal might make a technology decision with which the lawyer is not comfortable. There are risks with any employee, especially one in a professional capacity.

The issue for the solo and small firm practitioner, however, is not risk and it is not trust. The truly successful solo practitioner knows that he or she cannot practice law productively without the assistance of really competent, professional staff members. The ability of one lawyer to do all of the jobs in the law firm successfully is not even a debatable concept. Aside from the issues of time management, the solo cannot possible have all of the skills or currency of information and knowledge to be effective in every role. Moreover, operating a law office in that model makes absolutely no economic sense because the person with the highest level of education and skills is performing at a level far below those skills. Having a trained, licensed lawyer engaged in filing documents, typing, purchasing office supplies, and verifying a bank statement, among other tasks, inverts the economic model of law firm management to minimize the time and focus of the lawyer and that minimizes firm income and success.

The most important aspect of the issue of trust is the need for the solo and small firm practitioners to understand the true value of a paralegal to the practice of law and to the success of the practice. A practice that cannot grow will not succeed. That type of practice may result in income but, with growth, that income is like a rollercoaster exhibiting a series of highs and lows and functioning solely on the ability of the lawyer even with the assistance of one or more clerical personnel to make all of the professional and technical decisions. The functioning of such an office is focused solely on the lawyer who must be all things professional. The result is fragmentation and the inability to plan, to anticipate, and to grow. Growth is not only a function of money and new cases but also a function of stimulating and challenging issues that help the lawyer move to a new level and to gain new expertise. That keeps the practice interesting and avoids the practice malaise that is common today.

By removing a group of tasks from the lawyer and giving them to a professional in the office serving as a legal assistant the lawyer is able to bring to bear those skills that maximize training and stimulate intellectual, economic, and professional growth. The paralegal can do this because the paralegal is trained to perform specific tasks at a level below that of the lawyer but above that of clerical staff. One other concern among lawyers is that a law student serving in the traditional "law clerk" position, or a new lawyer serving as an associate, can better provide the professional support in the law office. That decision depends to some degree on the level of the law practice. Where the practice is generating new legal matters with a lot of variety, the associate can provide valuable assistance in the actual delivery of the legal services. To some degree, the law student can also serve in that role, especially if he or she is nearing the end of law school. However, that advantage quickly evaporates without the professional services provided by a paralegal. There are two reasons. First, the associate and the law student are unlikely to remain with the law firm for very long. Unless the firm grows at a sufficiently high level, the associate is going to develop professionally and move on because the economics of supporting two lawyers depends almost entirely on exponential growth. Clearly the law student is also like to leave or at best to become an associate again for a relatively short term.

The paralegal is much more likely to stay for a significantly longer period of time because the opportunity in the law firm represents professional growth and the use of skills. The paralegal invests in the firm and, unless there is something unexpected or a lack of opportunity for growth, the paralegal will stay. That means continuity and expertise in the operation of the firm that supports the activities of the lawyer. That also means the lawyer will not have to expend the capital, economic and temporal, to constantly rehire and retrain professionals. Finally, the work of the paralegal is not the work that a new associate or law clerk is willing or trained to perform. Both will do a little bit of typing of course and "help out" with some activities; but they are not willing to do those things for the long term. The paralegal views the spectrum of activities in a law firm as the professional role. The investment in a paralegal is going to pay a variety of dividends to the firm on a long-term basis, as opposed to the short-term gains of an associate or law clerk.

There is no doubt that when a solo or small firm practitioner takes the step to hire a paralegal, there are some risks. For that step to be successful and to result in the types of gains outlined above, the lawyer must engage in planning for that success. The reality is that the lawyer should be engaging in that type of long-range planning anyway. A lawyer whose management is purely reactive is much less likely to have a firm that really succeeds. The paralegal brings a richness of skills, knowledge of technology, and exposure to law and procedure to the law firm. But, most of all, the paralegal brings an enthusiasm that comes from the opportunity for growth and professional development. For the paralegal, the law firm is a cornucopia of long-term opportunity and for the lawyer that very cornucopia offers measured success for the law firm in the short and long term. To give that up for control or because of risk or because of trust is to lose that very success.

14 The Ethics of Working with Legal Assistants

by Therese A. Cannon

Paralegals play an important and substantive role in law practice. They work directly with clients and others involved in client matters. They draft, summarize, and organize legal documents. They often have a large part in preparing cases for trial. Many paralegals work quite autonomously, exercising a good deal of independent judgment in performing their work. In carrying out their responsibilities, paralegals often encounter ethical issues and need skills in the following areas:

- Knowing the ethics rules.
- Identifying ethical dilemmas when they arise.
- Applying knowledge of the rules to the situation at hand.
- Solving ethical problems—knowing what to do in the immediate context and when to refer a problem on to a lawyer or someone else in the firm for resolution or further action.

- Accessing strong support for ethical conduct within the office, in the form of firm ethics policies and procedures and a culture of ethical conduct.

Nearly all states have adopted some version of Rule 5.3 of the American Bar Association Model Rules of Professional Conduct, which outlines how lawyers are responsible for the ethical conduct of the nonlawyers they employ. This rule requires partners, lawyers with comparable managerial authority, and law firms "to make responsible efforts to ensure that the firm has in effect measures giving reasonable assurance" that paralegals' actions are compatible with the lawyer's ethical obligations. A lawyer is ethically responsible for misconduct if he or she ordered the action or ratified it with knowledge; or if he or she is a partner, has comparable managerial authority, or supervises the person, and knew of the conduct and failed to take remedial action at a time when its consequences could have been mitigated or avoided.

Delegation and Supervision

Developing good skills of delegation and supervision is critical to being successful in law practice and to ensuring that ethical and performance standards are met. Poor delegation and supervision can result in substandard work product, missed deadlines, dissatisfied clients, and possibly ethical breaches.

Delegating and supervising paralegals entail the following responsibilities:

- Selecting qualified persons with appropriate general education, paralegal education, and experience. Paralegals who have completed a formal paralegal education at an ABA-approved paralegal program have had ethics instruction, in both a specific course and the general context of studying various practice areas.
- Matching a paralegal's skill set with the task that needs to be done. Assigning work to a paralegal who is not trained to do that specific work can be as ineffective and risky as hiring an unqualified person.

- Establishing orientation and training programs that teach paralegals about the firm's policies, procedures, and performance. This includes ethics instruction, policies, and resources. At least 25 states have adopted guidelines for the ethical utilization of paralegal services. Many of these follow the ABA Guidelines for the Utilization of Legal Assistant Services, which were first adopted by the ABA in 1991. If your state has guidelines, these should be in your training materials. You may want to include the ABA guidelines as well. The two major paralegal associations, the National Association of Legal Assistants and the National Federation of Paralegal Associations, also publish codes of ethics.
- Outlining clear practices and procedures for delegating assignments to paralegals. A standard form e-mail or memorandum should be sent to the paralegal with each project. If the paralegal receives assignments verbally, adopt a standard form to which information concerning the assignment can be transferred for confirmation of the instructions. Among the items that should be covered in delegating work are the name of the client and matter and case number, if relevant; billing information or references; specific work that is being delegated; deadline for completion; estimate of the amount of time the task should take; references to resources or persons needed to complete the project; copies to others working on the client matter; and a special notation if the assignment is urgent.
- Reviewing the paralegal's work. The degree and level of that review depends, of course, on the nature of the work and the paralegal's qualifications to do the assigned work. If a paralegal is drafting a document with minor changes from a standard form, the lawyer does not have to read every word to determine that the document is properly drafted. But if a paralegal is drafting a complex document for the first time, a careful and thorough reading is needed.
- Evaluating through a formal process the quality of the paralegal's work and general level of productivity. This should be done at least annually and can be greatly enhanced by reviewing the feedback provided regularly as work is done and projects are completed.

Unauthorized Practice of Law

Unauthorized practice of law is prohibited in nearly every state. And every jurisdiction has an ethics rule like Model Rule 5.5 of the ABA Model Rules of Professional Conduct, which prohibits lawyers from aiding in the unauthorized practice of law.

The general rule is that a nonlawyer cannot do any of the following three things:

1. Appear in court on behalf of a client.
2. Establish the attorney-client relationship.
3. Give legal advice.

Court appearances. A nonlawyer cannot represent a client in a court of law. The prohibition on court appearances by nonlawyers specifies two important types of appearances:

- Depositions. A paralegal cannot take a deposition, even if armed with a set of lawyer-approved questions, and cannot represent the interests of a client at a deposition by advising a client whose deposition is being taken. Paralegals may attend depositions to assist lawyers and to observe (i.e., to assess the demeanor of a witness).
- Pleadings. A paralegal cannot sign a pleading on behalf of a client because the filing of a pleading constitutes an appearance.

The exceptions to the court appearance rules are confined to the following three circumstances:

- Federal law allows federal administrative agencies to set the qualifications of persons who appear before them as advocates. Some agencies require that representatives be lawyers; most do not. States are split; some follow federal practice, and others hold that administrative agency advocacy is "the practice of law" and therefore requires representatives to be lawyers. States that allow nonlawyer practice before state administrative agencies also allow a nonlawyer who is lawyer-supervised to act as an advocate at hearings.

- All states participate in practical training programs that allow qualified law students registered under the program to make court appearances with lawyer supervision.
- Some enlightened courts have established local rules that allow paralegals who are registered with the court to make nonadversarial ministerial appearances before them on behalf of local lawyers.

Undertaking representation. Neither a paralegal nor any other nonlawyer may establish the lawyer-client relationship by deciding whether the lawyer will undertake representation and/or by determining the fee arrangement. Lawyers have been severely disciplined for allowing paralegals to have clients sign retainer agreements without their having met the lawyer and without the lawyer's having reviewed and assessed whether representation was appropriate.

Legal advice. Giving legal advice includes any of the following:

- Directing or recommending a course of action with legal consequences.
- Explaining to a person his or her legal rights and responsibilities.
- Evaluating the probable outcome of a legal matter.
- Interpreting statutes, decisions, and legal documents for a person.
- Preparing legal documents for someone by applying knowledge of the law to the specific situation.

Firm policies should clearly prohibit paralegals from discussing legal matters like those detailed above. If a client asks such a question, the paralegal should restate that they cannot give legal advice and will check with the lawyer for an answer. To avoid confusion, introduce the paralegal to the client early on in the legal process. Explain the nature of the paralegal's involvement in the case, including the benefits to the client of working with a paralegal and the limits on the paralegal's authority to give legal advice.

Paralegals do have a major role to play in dealing with clients despite these restrictions because most communication with clients does not require the dispensing of legal advice; a lot of the contact simply keeps the client informed about the status of the case. If a paralegal refers a client's question to the attorney and later must relay an answer, the paralegal should be specifically delegated the task of communicating the advice to the client and must not alter or expand on the advice in any way. The paralegal should confirm this matter in writing in the file in the event that this delegation is made orally.

Outside Communications

Paralegals may communicate with judges, court personnel, witnesses, employees of clients, opposing counsel, and even opposing parties. To avoid confusion, all paralegals, especially those involved with litigation, must be made aware of the restrictions on the nature and content of such communications. The following rules should be specifically incorporated into firm policies:

- Paralegals should not have ex parte communications with judges about the subject matter of an ongoing case.
- Paralegals who uncover such adverse controlling authority in research must report it to the supervising lawyer so it can be properly addressed in documents filed with a court.
- Paralegals must be aware of rules prohibiting the introduction of false evidence and unlawfully obstructing access to or destroying or concealing evidence or witnesses.
- Paralegals should not communicate with jurors before or during a trial.
- Paralegals must not mislead witnesses and unrepresented persons regarding whose interests the lawyer represents. They should refrain from advising anyone they come into contact with about their legal rights and responsibilities.
- Paralegals may not communicate with opposing represented persons unless the contact is for the purpose of getting a second opinion or seeking new counsel.

Confidentiality

Protecting the confidentiality of client information is the responsibility of everyone in the law firm, particularly paralegals, who have so much access to client information. Policies to protect client information should be included in policy manuals and strictly adhered to.

In addition to standard procedures concerning files and computer security, firm policies should address issues arising from new technology, such as restrictions on sending electronic materials to opposing counsel and others; measures to ensure that previous drafts cannot be electronically accessed; restrictions on the recipients of e-mail communications sent to clients and others; and policies for forwarding confidential e-mails. Because of the major role paralegals have in document production, careful instructions should be given and oversight exercised in handling document productions to avoid the inadvertent disclosure of privileged documents. Paralegals should sign confidentiality agreements that prohibit them from revealing client information and set forth penalties for breach of that commitment, including termination of employment.

Conflicts of Interest

The conflicts rules generally apply to paralegals and other nonlawyers in much the same way they apply to lawyers. Therefore, a paralegal cannot work on opposite sides of an ongoing matter and cannot work on a matter adverse to a former client if the two matters are substantially related and confidentiality is therefore jeopardized. Conflicts also can arise for paralegals as a result of familial relationship with lawyers and other paralegals or as a result of their owning stock or having other business interests in a client's business.

In addition, through the principle of vicarious disqualification, most kinds of conflicts are imputed to everyone in the firm, thereby disqualifying the whole firm. However, the principle of vicarious disqualification has been applied more flexibly to paralegals.

The following preliminary steps should be taken when a paralegal is being hired:

- Paralegals should be screened for conflicts at the time that the firm makes an offer of employment.
- When a potential conflict is discovered, the firm must decide how to address the situation in a way that protects client confidentiality and prevents disqualification of the firm. The options

include obtaining consent from the affected clients, erecting a screen to protect against the communication of confidential information, and not employing or retaining the paralegal who has the conflict.

Nearly all states allow the screening of paralegals in situations where the screening of a lawyer would not be allowed. Setting up a screen involves:

- A written agreement signed by the paralegal, indicating that he or she will not reveal any confidential information about the matter in question.
- Written communications to lawyers and all other personnel advising them about the screen and admonishing them not to discuss the matter with the affected paralegal.
- Obvious markings on client files that indicate the existence of the conflict, restrictions on access to the files, and comparable limits on access to electronic records.
- Storage of affected files in a secure place, possibly not in the usual file room.
- Restricting the paralegal from working on the team assigned to the case, or in the same physical area, if possible.

The state of Nevada does not allow the screening of paralegals if a lawyer could not be similarly screened under the rules. Case law in Kansas has also been interpreted this way. A 1988 ABA ethics opinion and the proposed new comment to ABA Model Rule 1.10 suggest that screening of nonlawyers, including paralegals, should be permissible in such cases.

Money Matters

Timekeeping and billing. Like others in the law firm, paralegals must follow careful procedures in keeping track of their time so that clients are not overbilled, billed for duplicate or excessive time, and the like.

Client funds and property. In small law firms it is common for the paralegal to handle client trust accounts. If this is the case in your firm, be sure that paralegals are informed about jurisdictional rules regarding client trust accounts, including the prohibition on commingling client and lawyer funds and the requirements for records. Some states do not allow nonlawyers to sign on client trust accounts. Paralegals who might be handling client property must be aware of their duties to keep property safe and to turn over property to clients promptly.

Paralegal compensation. Lawyers may not split fees with paralegals but may have a compensation plan that includes bonuses or other amounts based on productivity and firm profitability. Referral fees are also strictly prohibited, as are partnerships between lawyers and nonlawyers for the practice of law.

Fee petitions. Under the landmark case *Missouri v. Jenkins* (491 U.S. 274 (1989)), the U.S. Supreme Court upheld a statutory award of attorney fees that included market-rate compensation for paralegal time. Since *Jenkins*, hundreds of cases have been decided in which fees for paralegal time were considered, giving guidance as to what must be included in a fee petition:

- The credentials of the paralegal. This includes formal college and paralegal education; voluntary certifications by the National Association of Legal Assistants (Certified Legal Assistant, Certified Legal Assistant Specialist) and National Federation Paralegal Associations (PACE Registered Paralegal); years of legal experience; and areas of expertise.
- Accurate and detailed time records.
- Information on market rates.

It should also be noted that courts often disallow fees requested for functions that are considered clerical or secretarial in nature or that are duplicative of work performed by someone else in the firm. Additionally, some courts will lower the rate of compensation if a lawyer does work that should have been delegated to a paralegal.

15 *Virtually Anything from a Virtual Paralegal or Legal Assistant*

by Lyza L. Sandgren

Here's the scenario. Your business has grown to the point that you can't do the work unless (1) you don't sleep or (2) you hire someone. Since you are already not sleeping, and you must find time to market your practice, you start looking for help.

You need someone with experience; someone who can hit the ground running and won't need much, if any, supervision. The problem is that an experienced secretary or paralegal is not easy to find and, when found, he or she invariably will want a good salary, healthcare, 401(k)s, sick leave, time or days off for child care, and paid vacations. Since you wish you had that too, someone experienced may not be feasible. Where is Erin Brockovich when you need her? So, you hire a temp, a recent paralegal school graduate, or someone equally inexperienced. Bad idea. They are worse than no help because they must be trained, which takes time—the thing you didn't have enough of in the first place. In addition, the work ethic may be marginal; they are often late and complain about not being near shopping. You even may have lost billable time trying to train your ex-employees.

Then, over drinks, a solo friend mentions using a "virtual" service. You know what that is—or do you? What is a "virtual" paralegal or assistant, and are they effective? Can you afford one? You need to grow your practice, but are they really an alternative to the full-time employee? And where are they? Hiding in plain sight on the Web.

With the advent of advanced technology and the local, state, and federal courts going electronic, many highly experienced paralegals and assistants, tired of dead-end jobs and the struggle to break through the "glass ceiling," struck out on their own. They built contract service organizations geared to helping the solo and small firm get the same, if not better, quality help and work product as the lawyer would have received from an in-house paralegal by utilizing their years of education, practical experience, and proven work ethic. Many did so well that they began hiring others with the same skills and a preference for working for themselves or from home. They became known as "virtual paralegals, receptionists or assistants." Today, you can get anything on a contract basis, from receptionists six states away answering your phones to highly specialized paralegals providing research and work product on the level of a multi-year associate.

There are more of these virtual services out in the ether than you may realize, and they can be found in every state. (I have seen too many problems arise from the use of off-shore, English-challenged virtual services, thus I am highlighting only U.S. virtual businesses here.) The virtual service offers the chance to get legal work done transactionally, with the lawyer paying only for the time it took to complete the project. Rates vary geographically and via practice area, but are also fair and provide room to build in a margin of profit. Since virtual paralegals and legal assistants are 1099 contractors, the lawyers who hire them don't have to worry about paying for healthcare, 401(k)s, sick days, short- or long-term medical leave, worker's compensation, paid vacations, or overtime.

Of course, the primary concern is always the work product. Can the work be trusted? In a word, yes! Since they are business owners as well as paralegals and want their businesses to succeed, they have a vested interest in client satisfaction. They also have the experience and training to write briefs; provide complex discovery and trial assistance; assemble trial binders; prepare formal filing papers, wills, bankruptcy and divorce papers, real estate filings, and documents; file electronic papers with organizations such as the U.S. Patent and Trademark Office or the World Intellectual Property Office; and perform complex legal research. In addition, most are qualified by education and experience to work with clients and experts.

So who are these masked men and women? To mention a few, let's start with the founding members of the newly formed American Freelance Paralegal Association (AFPA). First up is David A. Moyer, freelance paralegal and owner of Moyer Paralegal Services (MPS), http://www.moyerparalegal.com, in Cuyahoga Falls, Ohio. MPS services include document preparation, legal and Internet research, and consumer protection issues. Moyer has 13 years of experience in bankruptcy law, business law, consumer law, family law, and wills and probate. Of virtual services, Moyer says, "MPS functions virtually through the "Can We Help?" page on our Web site. It allows clients to write a detailed request for services, leaving their contact information. Our office can then work with them through e-mail, phone or fax. This way, we can work virtually with clients throughout the United States and the rest of the world."

On the West Coast is R.J. Morris, certified paralegal who has 17 years of legal, administrative, management, and organizational experience. After working with an Orange County, California, law firm for 12 years as paralegal, civil litigation case manager, and head of the commercial collection department, she ventured out and founded Impartial Inc., www.impartialinc.com, where she now serves as CEO, managing offices in California and Nevada. Impartial specializes in discovery assistance with over 15 years of collection and business litigation experience. While Impartial handles all collection litigation matters, they pride themselves on their work with construction default litigation. Impartial can provides its clients with specialized discovery for specific litigation matters, including a complete case analysis in client-ready format for the lawyer's approval. The analysis will not only include a summary of the facts and documents, it will also include additional discovery recommendations where the case is lacking in potential and settlement recommendations. She is adamant about her company's work, saying, "With properly handled discovery, clients can be advised as to the advantages or disadvantages of their litigation and potential outcome."

"Virtual paralegals offer all types of services from legal to administrative," Morris continues, "ensuring that client lawyers have the exact same benefit of an in-house paralegal, but for a fraction of the cost."

Freelancers can provide anything from word processing and dictation to complex discovery and trial assistance. Investigate freelance paralegals in your area and you will find they can do default packages, as well as prepare bankruptcy and divorce pleadings and documents.

Virtual service providers must be as diligent about their ethics and education as they are about their work product, and Marsha Kopan is a prime example. She is a certified paralegal and certified real estate support specialist and has earned her certified virtual assistant designation from the International Virtual Assistants Association (IVAA), http://www.ivaa.org.

Kopan has not one but three virtual businesses in West Allis, Wisconsin: Executive Secretarial Services, http://www.execsecsrv.com; MKEParalegal, http://www.mkeparalegal.com; and Association Management Resources, http://www.associationmanagementresources.com. She says, "Whether you are just starting your legal practice or your office is swamped with work, outsourcing to an independent paralegal service is cost-effective. No payroll headaches, no equipment to purchase, no desk space to provide, no retraining the turnover of temporary staff, is the way to solve a variety of logistical issues." Her paralegal practice focuses on business and real estate law, and she also provides complete office management services.

Jeannie Johnston, nationally known founder and operator of the Paralegal Gateway, the largest Paralegal information portal on the World Wide Web, recently said, "With over 50,000 clicks per month, ParalegalGateway.com has become a central source for Paralegals across the globe. Thanks to local associations and publications such as *Legal Assistant Today*, Paralegals are now, more than ever, beginning to receive the recognition they deserve." When Johnston was tapped to become a director of the AFPA, her response was more than enthusiastic: "I am thrilled and honored to have been asked to join an organization that supports the freelance paralegal business owner. The virtual business is here to stay."

In addition, virtual support is not only provided by paralegals. There are virtual receptionists, such as Ruby Receptionist, http://www.

callruby.com, with a proven track record of quality service and cost-effectiveness; Perceptionist, Inc., www.myperceptionist.com, one of the fastest-growing virtual receptionist and secretarial services in the United States; and Virtual Receptionists USA, www.virtualreceptionist.biz, giving a lot of corporate service for the buck. You get the client comfort of having a person answer your phone rather than impersonal voicemail, and many offer secretarial and other bundled business services.

As more and more lawyers become emboldened to use experienced, virtual service providers rather than hire inexperienced in-house support, more and more legal professionals will stop worrying about how the work will get done and get some sleep, or even plan an actual vacation. Who knows? They might even be able to leave the BlackBerry at home . . . Nah!

Part V
Rules of Engagement

Does your secretary really understand what "attorney-client relationship" and "client confidentiality" mean? The casual introduction to those concepts when you hired the secretary can easily lapse into lip service with time and tempting circumstances. Reinforce the concept. Your staff needs continuing refresher courses just as much as you require continuing legal education to keep those synapses wired to concepts, old and new. Renewing these "soft" skills is more important than upgrading your computer's word processing program. Now is the time to tend the home fires.

Chapter 18
Legal Staff Evaluations: A Generational Issue as Well
by Ted A. Wagoner

Chapter 19
Workplace Security for Solo and Small Firm Staff
by David Zachary Kaufman

Beyond the Employee Handbook: Personal Issues

16

by Jean Maneke

When you are a solo or in a small firm, the idea of strict job descriptions and hard lines between duty assignments often disappears. You know that you are the senior partner and the janitor. You come in on weekends to get work done for clients and sometimes during the week have to take time out to inspect copiers and decide which one to purchase.

The same thing is true of your staff. Your paralegal, legal assistant, or trusted secretary sometimes is researching the proper form for a client. Other times, he or she may be ordering office supplies. And still other times, he or she is essentially running your office while you are unavailable, either in trial or on vacation.

Because of the important role this person plays in your life, you can sometimes find yourself in a close personal relationship. It happens regardless of your desire to keep an employer/employee relationship. You know of the times this person has bailed you out of a difficult situation and you are grateful. As a result, you try to be equally benevolent when this person needs a break. The strict rules of boss and subordinate tend to become fuzzy. And that's when difficulties start.

Maybe you begin feeling this person is taking advantage of you in terms of time away from the office. Maybe you feel guilty insisting that vacation or sick leave be taken according to your office policy. Perhaps you discover that your assistant has taken your desire to accommodate your clients too greatly to heart and is now establishing a close personal relationship with a client, which could be troubling to you in terms of client confidentiality. Or perhaps you suddenly discover that, in response to a tale of woe a staff member has shared with a client, the client has made a personal loan to the staff person, putting your employee in a compromised position and jeopardizing your ethical relationship with that client.

Handling the relationship between yourself and your staff can be extremely difficult for a solo or member of a small firm. In a large firm, the staff administrator handles all personal matters regarding staff, and the attorney need only supervise assignments that are given to an employee assigned to that attorney. The attorney need not be concerned with the staffer's personal life or with whether individual issues will interfere with performance of the job; the staffer is told to contact the staff administrator regarding personal issues, and the staff administrator then arranges for another staff person to take over accomplishing the attorney's assignment.

Oh, to have all those layers of supervision as a small firm or solo lawyer. No such luck, though. When your secretary's child develops a major illness, you know that you are going to be working without a secretary for some time. When your receptionist goes on vacation and you have no other staff person, you'll be answering the door when the delivery persons arrive, interrupting whatever else you have going on at the moment.

That is one reason why a staff employee manual or handbook is a critical tool for a small office. Because of that personal relationship and because there is a tendency to want to be accommodating to an employee who is valuable, you will find you are squeezed when tough questions arise. How do you decide whether to give this person extra time off? How do you decide what a personal leave policy should amount to in any given year? How do you know what policies you will follow before you fire a person who has pushed you further than you think you can stand and still run a functional office?

It is true that a small office allows you to have some flexibility in work conditions. When you think about handbooks, you probably think about large companies that set rules in stone for employees and where there is no personal interface between employer and employee. But while having some flexibility is good, it is also important to set out some basic rules so that there is a consistent baseline for office interactions and operations.

The handbook should set out a number of policies that are basic work-related decisions. First, it should state that policies can only be changed in writing, so that if you ever get into a dispute with a staff person, you are protected from the "he said/she said" dispute. And, no matter how close you find yourself with your employees, the day will come when you will decide that you have reached the end of your rope with one of them and that they must be fired. And when that day comes, your written records are what will save you, *not* what either of you might have said.

Further, if you are in an "employment at will" state, you need to be sure to say that nothing in the handbook creates an employment contract. In addition, you should either consult with a lawyer specializing in employment law or satisfy yourself that you have included all language relating to equal employment rights and other worker rights laws.

This is the place to set out in detail what the hours are for the position and your policy regarding overtime work and pay. Be sure you add a sentence that employees are expected to be punctual in their arrival at work and that tardiness is a terminable offense. Despite the fact that you may occasionally overlook a tardy employee who has a personal issue at that time, you will find your patience wearing thin when coming in late is an everyday occurrence. It is also a good practice to set out employee benefits, either in the handbook or in an attachment.

If you live in an area of the country whether inclement weather creates issues, you need to decide what your policy will be for such situations. For example, in the Midwest, where I practice, snowfalls can come suddenly and heavily, and unexpected and severe weather conditions discourage anyone from driving anywhere. I, of course, will end up staying at work until the work is done because I have no choice, or, if I am fortunate enough to have taken something home that needs to be done, I may choose to work at home until I finish the task and until the roads are in better condition. But I assure you that for the boss, taking a day off work is probably not an option.

Your employee, however, is likely to have other emotional responses to such weather conditions. Suddenly, when the schools call "snow days," your employee may have child-care problems, or may decide that he or she misses those good old days when you could stay home and watch soap operas or play Monopoly all day while drinking cocoa. Now, none of us are comfortable insisting staff drag themselves in through a foot of snow and take a chance on wrecking the family car. But a run of snow days can put any business out of business when suddenly the normal allowed vacation is doubled because you, as the boss, have graciously allowed an employee extra days off due to the weather. I can personally testify to the frustration of being out of town, far away from the weather in question, and having to make a judgment call as to whether weather conditions in a town hundreds of miles away warrant granting staff a snow day. One possible way to avoid this whole issue is to allow staff to use their vacation/sick leave to cover a "snow day" if they prefer to stay home, but make it clear that there will be no additional vacation/sick time allowed beyond that granted to each employee in the handbook. Removing the stress of having to make that call early in the morning, especially when *you* know that you will be in the office because something has to be done and there's no one but you to do it, removes some of the resentment from such a day.

Further, if you allow an employee to use vacation and sick leave for various other purposes, your handbook needs to be clear that being absent from work without leave is a terminable offense. Otherwise, you are liable to find that employees will just assume that if they don't want to work, they can stay home without pay and yet continue to be employed when they choose to work. You need employees who show up at work on a regular basis that you can depend on. In addition, it is important to explain in the handbook how vacation time is earned and available to the employee. This is probably one of the most important issues to address and to make certain that it makes sense; if there is anything that is subject to multiple interpretations in this language, you, the employer, are going to find it is being interpreted against you by the employee.

Obviously, it is wise to set out in advance what holidays the office recognizes, because it allows your employees to plan in advance for when they'll be off, especially for major holidays like Thanksgiving and Christmas. And it allows you to simply say, "Let's check the handbook" when an employee asks if he or she is off for a certain holiday. At the same time, it is wise to add a sentence that management retains the right to announce other closures if they desire. Sometimes you will want a three-day holiday, and if the workload has been heavy, you'll want to give staff an extra day off, too. But the goal is to stick to the set holidays in most cases, so the staff knows when they can expect a vacation from work.

Sometimes a staff member will struggle with what to do with a child if that child cannot stay home alone during work hours. For such situations, it is advisable to have a set policy regarding children coming to work with their parent. In some cases, because you are in a smaller firm, accommodations can be made for such situations. Perhaps you have a back room where you can keep a television and sleeping bag and accommodate a sick child. Your staff will love you forever if you can do that. At the same time, older children are a challenge in a small office. If the child is sick, you have no desire to spread illness among you and other staff members, let alone your clients. You may worry that clients will view the firm as unprofessional if they see children running around in the office. (How many large firms allow parents to babysit children at their work stations? Probably none on a regular basis.) And frankly, what is the likelihood that your staff member will be able to focus and get work done if a child is hanging around his or her desk? These are questions that require soul searching, but it seems wise to resolve these issues in some fashion and have a policy concerning such matters in your handbook so that staff members do not repeatedly ask you about bringing their children to work.

Use of cell phones at work is a mixed blessing, too. Requiring staff to make personal calls on their own cell phones keeps your office lines free of personal calls and helps keep costs down for you in terms of having lines free for clients' use, while limiting the number of phone lines you require for your business. At the same time, unlimited access to personal cell phones can mean unlimited access to personal phone calls, and, if unchecked, that can result in a significant drain on employees' time. Therefore, it seems prudent to have a statement in your employee handbook about the need to keep personal phone calls limited so that they do not interfere with employees' doing the job they've been hired to do.

Another issue in terms of professionalism is employee attire. In summer, an employer struggles with the degree of bareness that one is comfortable with. In winter, an employer struggles with the degree of casualness one is comfortable with, especially when the weather is ugly. While it is true that in a small office, one's relationship with clients may be more informal than in a large firm, it is also true that if professionalism is a critical issue for the solo or small firm practitioner, the attire of the lawyer and of staff members is a significant component of that image. Some lawyers can pull off dressing outside the "dress for success" style and have a client base that looks beyond that personal peccadillo. But for most of us, the way we look and the way our office and staff look are key factors in the trust our clients place in us. Your staff needs to understand why you insist on a professional appearance. Similarly, it is important that they understand that the appearance of their work space contributes to this office appearance and that you expect them to keep their work space under control, particularly if it is an area where clients may be present. In addition, this helps maintain the confidence of clients that their confidential information is not out where a casual passer-by might see it.

Client confidentiality is a critical issue to address in your handbook. Employees must be told in a pointed matter that they are never to discuss personal client information with any other person and that doing so will subject them to immediate termination. But I also suggest that if you allow an employee to develop a personal relationship with a client, you are jeopardizing the security of your office and creating a conflict of interest between you and your employee. While this presents difficult issues in a small community, it is important for a lawyer to understand all the relationships between your staff and your clients. If you cannot trust an employee to put your interests before all others in their job duties, then you need to terminate that employee. If an employee is caught accepting a substantial gift from a client, I would suggest you have a significant conflict present, and for that reason, I think it is critical to warn all employees that gifts in excess of Internal

Revenue Service guidelines ($25) are a violation of your staff policy.

Similarly, employees need to understand that there is no right of confidentiality to anything in their office computer, particularly in regard to their e-mail. Downloaded games, programs, and music are to be prohibited, due to copyright, spam, and virus issues.

Sometimes these steps seem harsh and unfriendly, and small firm or solo practitioners will feel that such a handbook doesn't create the intimate, friendly feeling that is desired in the office. But being a lawyer is a profession, and your professional reputation is your most important possession. When there is confusion between you and your staff, your reputation is harmed at its most sensitive point—your most critical relationship. Your clients sense the attitude your staff has toward you. The relationship between your employees and your clients is critical to your reputation. Being professional on every level is one of the most important steps you can take to maintain that reputation with your clients.

17 Internet, E-mail, and Computer Policies for the Small Law Office

by Robin Page West

Technology has leveled the playing field so that small and mid-size law firms now compete with ease against the behemoths. Some enterprising and nimble-fingered solo practitioners even function without secretaries now that e-mail and portable document format obviate the need for staff to lick envelopes and operate photocopy and fax machines. The productivity gains occasioned by modern technology, though, can easily be eclipsed by losses due to cyberslacking and outright computer misuse and abuse.

A secretary in one small law firm was complaining that her computer was too old and slow. Indeed, it was an older machine without much RAM or hard drive space by current standards, but it was nevertheless more than adequate to do her job, which consisted only of typing documents in Word. Even though the computer was connected to the Internet, this particular secretary had been specifically admonished not to go online, in part because of her time management and focus problems and in part because the computer was not as robust as it should have been for online use. One day the computer completely froze and the secretary announced, "See, I told you I needed a new computer!" A little excavation around her hard drive revealed that a slew of temporary files, data miners, and cookies from a host of retailers of women's apparel had taken up what remaining free space existed and caused the computer to lock up.

Does she have cause to be indignant that the firm snooped into her Internet use? She wants to know what the difference between that is and, for example, her boss surreptitiously listening in on her personal phone calls. An Internet policy prohibiting staff use of the firm's equipment for personal Internet shopping, containing a statement that the firm may monitor an employee's Internet use, would go a long way toward clarifying the firm's expectations and the secretary's job description.

"Despite the small-firm penchant for a more relaxed atmosphere, many law practice management consultants believe that all firms should have a written Internet policy. At the very least, employees should be on notice that they have no privacy rights in their electronic activities, including communications, and that certain behavior will subject them to discipline or dismissal," writes Ann Sherman, *Small Firm Business,* May 11, 2006 (http://www.law.com/jsp/law/sfb/lawArticleFriendlySFB.jsp?id=1147251928671).

Many people like to participate in listservs, which are groups of people who post messages on the Internet that are automatically sent to everyone else on the list. Listservs can generate hundreds of e-mails or more in a single week. These e-mails take time to read and write and computer space to store them. When users post a comment, it is automatically disseminated to everyone else on the list, and the comment will be, in many cases, searchable by the public. Law firms should consider whether to allow staff to participate in listservs on firm time, using the firm domain name and equipment.

"According to the 2nd annual survey by America Online and Salary.com, the average worker admits to squandering 1.86 hours per 8-hour workday, not including lunch and scheduled break-time. . . . The biggest distraction for respondents was personal Internet use. 52.0% of the 2,700 people polled cited web surfing as their #1 distraction at work," write Dan Malachowski and Jon Simonini on Salary.com (http:/

/aolsvc.salary.aol.com/careersandwork/salary/articles/atcl_career advice.asp?atc=573).

Another form of Internet communication is instant messaging (IM). Tools such as AOL Instant Messenger, Google Talk, and others (available for free download) allow computer users to type messages to each other in real time, which is faster than e-mail. Sometimes these programs come preloaded on new computer.

According to Dan Pinnington in his article "Managing the Security and Privacy of Electronic Data in a Law Office—Part III" (http://www.abanet.org/lpm/lpt/articles/tch03052.html), "IM products have little or no encryption or security, so IM statements are public and can expose your office to embarrassment. As well, IM makes it very easy to download or share files across the Web, and thus opens the doors for viruses. . . . IM can have a useful business purpose, but at present, it is usually used for personal conversations by office staff, often without permission. When using IM, it actually looks like staff is working hard on their computers. Most law offices will want to prohibit the use of IM in their technology use policy."

Issues of cyberslacking aside, technology can create as many new problems as it solves. Whether inattention, ineptitude, or urgency causes the mistakes initially, the problem is that technology magnifies them. In a second, one small goof can be transmitted to an unlimited number of recipients. The extra buffer time afforded by paper communications that had to be proofread, signed, copied, folded, and placed in an envelope does not exist for their electronic counterparts.

A firm Internet/e-mail policy is one way to rein in the little missteps that occur during the daily operation of a law firm and that can become major headaches when technology compounds them. The policy is a way to anticipate the problems before they occur and to raise consciousness in the office so that if they do occur, everyone realizes it and knows how to take corrective action.

Where I practice in Baltimore, people first started taking these kinds of issues seriously back in the eighties during the asbestos litigation after a legal secretary faxing a privileged and confidential memo to a joint defense committee of big-firm lawyers mistakenly pressed the pre-programmed "fax blast" button for scores of plaintiffs' lawyers instead (or was it the other way around?) and triggered months of *tsuris* for everyone involved. Legal periodicals and intra-firm memos analyzed whether the faxed document had lost its privileged status, or whether, conversely, the receiving lawyers who read the inadvertent transmission had committed an ethical *faux pas* by doing so. Virtually every lawyer and legal secretary in town was thinking "Wow, glad it was not me/my secretary who pressed that button!" It would be hard to quantify how many hours counsel and the court were sidetracked sorting this one out while the asbestosis victims awaited their day in court.

Today's equivalent of the fax blast is the mass-mailing feature that allows a sender to e-mail an unlimited number of recipients the same message with a single flick of the finger. I find it irksome to receive messages prominently displaying my e-mail address in the list of 50 other recipients. Who are all those other recipients, and what are the chances that they will now click to add me to their list of people to whom they send funny jokes and tearjerker chain letters that I am not the least bit interested in?

Bear in mind, too, that if your firm sends out mass mailings, such as client newsletters, via e-mail, your recipient clients may also not appreciate having their identities broadcast in this manner. The last thing someone who quietly consulted a matrimonial lawyer for pre-divorce advice wants to see is her name on a client newsletter mailing list. Make sure your staff understands that regardless of what you send clients, whether it's legal advice or a firm newsletter, client identity should not be disclosed to others. Sending the mass-mailed message to yourself and putting all other recipients' addresses in the "bcc" field rather than in the "to" field solves this problem nicely by keeping everyone's identity (except the sender's) hidden.

The flip side to the problem of obliviously publicizing the e-mail addresses of people who might prefer to remain anonymous is attaching a sender's name to something he did not send. This can happen, for example, when a firm employee receives an e-mail containing the genuine, confidential chocolate chip cookie recipe billed as having been stolen directly from Mrs. Fields' Cookies. The recipe is mouth-watering, your secretary can't imagine it is really stolen, and even if it is, so what? She knows her friends would love to have it. So with a few keystrokes, your secretary forwards the e-mail, and your law firm has just sent 20 people you don't even know a stolen trade secret. As in the case of listserv postings, the firm name has been associated with communications it may not even be aware of.

Jim Calloway, director of the Oklahoma Bar Association Management Assistance Program, observes:

> [I]f the law firm has its own domain name, all outgoing e-mails might be assumed to be the equivalent of communications on law firm stationery. This could be embarrassing if the e-mail is forwarded to others. Different policies might then be needed for the receptionist whose outgoing e-mail announces it is from mary@Fredslawfirm.com as opposed to mary.smith@sbcglobal.com. A few years ago corporate America became quite concerned about employees wasting company time on the Internet and many businesses banned employees accessing Web-based e-mail services like Hotmail and Yahoo. While I understand that point of view, I would also make the point that I'd probably prefer an employee do that and not use my domain name if they sent out a lot of personal e-mail. (http://www.okbar.org/members/map/articles/malpractice.htm)

Another stealth screw-up is the "autofill" feature that automatically completes an e-mail address after the author types in the first few letters. If both your client and your opposing counsel's e-mail addresses begin with the same few letters, you or your staff may inadvertently send client communications to your adversary. Always double-check the e-mail's recipients before hitting "send," or, better yet, disable the autofill feature on your office computers.

And then there's the whole metadata problem. Metadata is information that an application saves automatically without the computer user even knowing it. For example, Word will store the first few words of a document as its "title" regardless of the title you give the document when you saved it, and the document will keep that title even if you later change those first few words in the document. What's more, you will not see this title when you open the document to read it on your screen or when you print it out. This title is hidden from view, yet readily accessible. Why is this significant? Suppose a new client, Alpha Technology, asks you to prepare a buy/sell agreement. You quote the firm's standard flat rate—$1,500. Alpha agrees and e-mails you all the information you need to start drafting. The next day you check with your partner to see if he has done a buy/sell recently and strike pay dirt. He's just done one for Fido Kennels that is almost word-for-word exactly what Alpha Technology will need.

You retrieve it from your firm's network, change its name to reflect that of the new client and make the other necessary changes substituting Alpha's information for Fido's. Total time: 20 minutes. You're feeling pretty smug because you know this is a top-notch buy/sell. Your partner is chair of the local bar association's business law committee, and he's 100 percent current on all aspects of this area of the law. You do a quick spell check and proofread, and e-mail the document in Word format to Alpha, knowing they are sure to be pleased with the fast turnaround.

But if someone from Alpha opens the document and then clicks on the "file" menu, and then on "properties," he or she will find out that the "title" of the document is Fido Kennels Buy/Sell, that it was authored not this week by you but by your partner last month, and that you only had the document open for a total of 20 minutes to edit it.

Not the best way to build credibility with a new client. Think this example is farfetched? Hardly. If I had to guess, I'd say most clients are far more computer-savvy than their lawyers, and can mine digital records for all kinds of information that we wouldn't have a clue about, such as revisions, comments by, and identities of other drafters, hidden text, and so on. Yet transmission of unintended data to clients may be the least of our worries. What if the document containing the prior versions and strategy commentary was something you sent to your adversary?

The ABA's electronic newsletter, *Your ABA*, has observed that "[m]any commentators urge lawyers to be extremely cautious when transmitting documents electronically, and suggest that they make full use of available software to 'scrub' metadata from them before they are sent. Some suggest that a lawyer has an affirmative duty to remove metadata." http://www.abanet.org/media/youraba/200601/article01.html. Microsoft's Web site has articles on how to minimize metadata from documents prepared with Word 97 (article ID 223790), Word 2000 (article ID 237361), Word 2002 (article ID 290945), and Word 2003 (article ID 825576). Metadata scrubbing software can automate this process first by alerting users to scrub a document before sending, and then by either blocking or removing the metadata. San Francisco–

based Workshare's Protect Enterprise Suite, Esquire Innovations' iScrub, BEC Legal Systems' Metadata Scrubber, JavaCool's Doc Scrubber, and Payne Consulting Group's Metadata Assistant are just a few of the popular applications that may prove helpful in plugging your office's metadata leaks.

Totally cleansing documents of all metadata is not always the best practice, however. Suppose a corporate client involved in a litigation matter produces documents requested in discovery in their native format, Word, to you on a CD. Using a metadata scrubber on them or otherwise changing the metadata before producing them could be the electronic equivalent of using white-out to delete information from a paper document. So, if you have trained your staff to delete all metadata, it behooves you also to explain to them that this rule does not necessarily apply to documents that are part of a litigation matter; cleansing of metadata in these records could be tantamount to destruction of evidence or spoliation, with serious consequences.

So the challenge is to provide firm employees access to technology together with guidelines for its use that minimize the potential for serious unintended consequences and for abuse. A law firm policy should be concise and easy to understand. It should spell out how firm employees may and may not use the firm equipment, that their use of firm equipment may be monitored, and that they should not expect communications made on firm equipment to be private. Following are some of the issues law firms must address in the course of developing an Internet and e-mail policy that strikes the right balance for each firm.

- Use of firm e-mail for personal communications
- Whether use of non-firm e-mail on firm equipment or firm time is permitted
- Use of firm e-mail for sending or forwarding jokes, chain letters, religious or political content
- Use of firm e-mail for transmitting legal advice
- Use of firm e-mail for Internet purchases
- Whether e-mail communications are considered private or whether the firm will monitor them

- Whether personal e-mails sent and received on firm equipment belong to the firm
- Liability of the firm for employees' personal data stored on the firm's equipment
- Expectation of privacy regarding data stored on the firm's equipment
- How long to keep firm e-mail, how and where to store it, and whether deletion is allowed or prohibited
- Guidelines for removal and preservation of metadata
- Participation in listservs/chat rooms and the retention policy for chat transcripts
- Confidentiality of data on office equipment
- Confidentiality of passwords
- Whether mass mailings require masking of recipients' identities

Formulating an Internet and e-mail use policy can be a painstaking process, and unfortunately there is no one-size-fits-all solution. But even an imperfect policy, revised over time, is better than none at all.

Legal Staff Evaluations

18

by Ted A. Wagoner

Why Perform Staff Evaluations?

Perry Mason had Della Street, and Arnie Becker had Roxanne Melman. Every lawyer has hoped for the day of employing the administrative assistant, secretary, paralegal, or office helper (in this article, staff) who always has the file ready to go, knows the calendar inside out, drafts pleadings and correspondence so they are ready to file with the first draft, and understands *The Blue Book: A Uniform System of Citation*™. At Peterson & Waggoner, LLP, we get close to that ideal state through coaching, training, and evaluation. This chapter explains how you can also get your office close, after a while.

Why should you evaluate employees, and what does that have to do with achieving a more competent staff and providing better legal services for the clients?

Being the supervisor of an associate lawyer, legal assistant, or staff member is an important responsibility. The performance of the duty of supervision is required to be performed by you, the lawyer. In addition, responsibility may rest with the supervising lawyer under your state's Rules of Professional Conduct.

David Maister, author of *True Professionalism,* describes the supervision as "a profound moral issue" and claims that diligence in supervising a client's transaction is "an ethical issue, a matter of responsibility for due care" and "true professionalism." Maister unfortunately concludes that "excellence in project supervision remains the exception rather than the rule."

You can supervise as a tyrant, you can be under the control of the staff member, or you can work together as a coach and team. There are dozens of styles for working together. The coach and team method of working is a great method that can be used to build a solid relationship that will help your firm to endure the trials of daily life in a law office. Due to the working relationship in most offices, you will need to be more of a player-coach, as you are also one of the members of the client's legal team. You may note that there are few player-coach models to learn from anymore, so we use the traditional coach model.

A good coach will point out mistakes made by the players during practice and during the game, because the coach wants to improve the performance of each player in order to improve the performance of the whole team. Successful evaluation is one critical aspect of successful coaching, and is therefore critical to the improvement of staff skills and efforts.

Are You Prepared to Evaluate?

Evaluation must be a continuous process. In preparing to evaluate, you need to focus on the ultimate goal, which is to determine that you have the right person doing the right job, based on the skill sets needed to perform that job. As Jim Collins says in *From Good to Great*, it is management's job to "have the right person in the right seat on the right bus."

In preparing to evaluate, there are several questions you must answer:

- Do you know the jobs that you want your staff to be doing?
- Does your staff know the jobs you want, and need, to have performed?

- Have you engaged in formal or informal training for those job duties?
- In small offices, each employee must perform a number of tasks every day. Is it reasonable to ask one person to be competent in those skills?
- Requiring excellence is appropriate, while requiring perfection is impossible. Have you decided what level of competence you expect?
- Have you discussed the competence requirements with the staff?
- Are you ready for generational differences between yourself and your staff?
- Do you have an evaluation tool to use in staff evaluations?

Staff evaluation is not especially effective or appropriate during periods of high frustration or great elation. Since the purpose of evaluation is to improve the process and program of your office practice, an evaluation during a period of disappointment may not be helpful to your staff or your relationship with them. Disappointing moments should be noted and analyzed soon after they occur, but it may be best to wait a couple days.

What to Evaluate

What talents do you prize most highly in your practice? What role does the staff have in developing the key indicators of what you prize? This is not a question of what they are best at, but of what is most needed by your office. Michael Corum says, "What you count is what counts." If the highest priority for your office is client relations, do you measure how your clients relate to the members of your staff and to you?

If you measure client satisfaction, do you accurately report that to the staff? If you do not measure the reactions of your clients, are you only projecting your uninformed thoughts when evaluating the staff's interaction with them?

Are you evaluating skill improvements? Drafting skills? The timely turnaround of legal documents? General attitude and aptitude? What evidence do you generate to back up your evaluation of these attributes? Skills that are important to your office and to your clients ought to be evaluated, and setting up the evaluation process is either your responsibility or a collaborative staff responsibility.

One current school of thought suggests that staff are "knowledge workers." According to noted management guru Peter Drucker, paralegals are among those considered knowledge workers. He says that they only become knowledge workers "through formal training and understanding of the theory and philosophy of the work they do." During the evaluation, are you testing the employee's understanding of the theory of the lawyer's role and the philosophy of your office practice? Are you providing for more formal training to build a staff member into a knowledge worker?

Evaluating in Light of Generational Differences

Law office staff members tend to reflect the sociological generation they belong to. Books abound on the effects these generational differences have, and a supervisor would be well advised to review some of this literature. Whether your employees are members of the Boomer generation, busters (often called Gen X), or Mosaics (this group is often called either Gen Y or the Millennials), each such group has certain common characteristics that very loosely help to define the generation. Earlier generations, such as Tom Brokaw's Greatest Generation—those born in the 1920s and early 1930s—and the Silent Generation, born in the mid-'30s through the end of World War II (also known as the Builders Generation), have their unique characteristics, but are retiring from the ranks of support staff.

Generally, boomers (those born between 1945 and 1965) were shaped by the loss of innocence in public life that started with the assassination of President Kennedy and culminated in 1968 with the assassinations of Martin Luther King, Jr. and Robert Kennedy, the Chicago Democratic convention, and the riots in large cities across the country. Overshadowing all those separate events was the war in Vietnam.

Boomers were raised by Builders to stay on a task, but also they tend to distrust decisions handed down by government leaders and other perceived authority figures. Decisions by common folk seem to be better or wiser than decisions made by so-called leaders, so all ideas from those in authority were to be considered suspect, and that included supervisors in the office. Collaborative decision making is acceptable, but authoritarian decisions are received with suspicion or hostility. Boomers took center stage in rebellion and do not seem to want to give it up.

Busters, or Gen Xers, who have been defined as those born from 1965 to 1983, are thus described by George Barna: "Busters took pride in their sloppy work habits, their disinterest in careers and their refusal to become educated simply to make a better living." These are generally not the credentials sought out by an employer. Dealing with such attitudes can be difficult, since the disinterest in careers can lead to shallow commitment to an employer. Employers' expectations of improvement in skills may result in resistance or resignation. This is where consistent coaching, rather than annual performance reviews, may work better. Incremental improvement on different areas of work may be more accepted than an expectation of large improvements that are only occasionally expressed.

Mosaics (named such by Barna) are stereotyped as those who "will likely baffle millions of people with their unpredictable, quixotic, seemingly inconsistent and idiosyncratic values, beliefs, attitudes and behaviors." Those values do not provide much promise about the style or quality of work Mosaics will likely provide a law office.

Rich Eynon, president of the Indiana State Bar Association, tells the tale of hiring two young (Mosaic) lawyers to work with him as he prepared to start his presidency. They assured him they were on board, but within months of his presidency taking effect, both younger lawyers decided to leave and head to another firm to pursue their individual dreams. Commitment to him or the firm was not a priority for either of them.

Eynon, a Boomer himself, was dumbfounded by such a cavalier and unprofessional attitude relative to how he defines a professional attitude. The lesson for us, though, is that legal employers and law office supervisors currently do not define professionalism the way the Builders defined it for the Boomers. As the younger generations use that term, its meaning has changed drastically.

You need to be aware that these differences are generally not seen to be "generational differences" by most. Most employees think of themselves as good people and don't understand why others are so different. As the employer and supervisor, you need to see and understand the basis for these differences as you are making staff evaluations.

When to Perform the Evaluation

Formal evaluations should be held on a regular basis. Most think of doing evaluations on either an annual or biannual timetable. If you use evaluations to influence wages, it makes sense to perform the evaluation when you are ready to adjust pay. Some disagree, thinking that pay decisions should be separate from evaluations, but I believe that the pay decision reinforces the findings in the evaluations.

Using the coaching metaphor suggested earlier, can you imagine a coach who starts the game but makes no suggestions, adjustments, or modifications until the start of the next game. Many lawyers do this in their staff evaluations. To avoid that kind of poor coaching, you should do a daily, or as-needed, evaluation. Like a coach, make the evaluation in reaction to an event.

When to Start the Evaluation Process

I had been practicing for 15 years when we first started formal staff evaluations. It was a difficult time for some members of the staff, including one who had been in the firm years longer than I had. Some staff members were concerned that the purpose of these evaluations was to force staff changes. We wanted to have changes, but not replacements. I did not do a good job of explaining the purpose or process for the evaluations.

In retrospect, we should have started evaluations as we brought on new staff, bringing long-term employees along more slowly; but we could not wait. If you have the opportunity, be prepared to start evaluations when you bring on that first assistant. Without that opportunity, start out with doing the informal daily evaluations as you find and fix mistakes in processes. Implement the formal evaluations after several weeks of open discussion during the informal daily or weekly evaluations.

How to Perform the Daily Evaluation

Daily evaluation sets the stage for the more formal evaluations. Responding to client compliments and concerns by promptly sharing them with the staff is important. It allows an opportunity to enjoy the compliment, or explain the complaint, and to suggest alternative ways to deal with the client in the future.

In performing an evaluation, daily or formal, you need to remember the training maxim popularized by Vince Lombardi: "You praise in public and correct in private."

Positive and negative comments made in a timely way will generally lead to a quicker, better result and to greater improvement by the staff member. Weekly and even daily moments for evaluative comments are important if growth and improvement in the employee's skills are the desired results.

Regular comments also reduce the tension around making negative comments. Corrective action can lead to defensiveness by staff or heightened aggravation for the lawyer.

How to Perform the Formal Evaluation

The first thing involved in performing an evaluation is to get mentally prepared. You can do that by taking the following steps:

- Tell the employee the evaluation is coming and provide the date and time;
- Provide the employee with a Self Evaluation form to fill out and return;
- Complete the Employer's Evaluation form prior to the meeting and before reviewing the completed Self Evaluation form.

While preparing for the evaluation, do the internal research necessary to be able to take another step in the development of the employee:

- Do the self evaluation and employer evaluation show an agreement about the need for further improvement?

- Can seminars or classes help in those areas where improvement is needed?
- Would specialized training do the job?
- Is a merit raise warranted? Cost of living adjustment is usually anticipated, but merit raises may require some justification.
- Is a bonus appropriate at this time?

It is important to be ready for questions from the staff about raises and bonuses. Staff usually know much more about the financial condition of the firm than the owners think. They see the bills go out and may see the checks come in. They know the cases we win and the ones we lose. Not being prepared for such questions can lead to some awkward moments, which can easily be misinterpreted.

After several years of doing twice-yearly evaluations and changing the evaluation form every time we did an evaluation, we came to the most effective method we have found yet.

A couple of days before we go through the evaluation process, we invite each staff member to perform a Self Evaluation on the same skill sets that we will use to evaluate the employee. It helps to facilitate the discussion and allows us to provide focused resources to strengthen weaknesses when we all recognize the same problems.

If there is a disagreement about the skill level of the employee, with the employee thinking he or she is either weaker or stronger than we have observed, we use that information to begin a discussion about our needs for training or for an opportunity for us to observe skills that we had overlooked.

We sit down with the employee with the evaluation forms in hand and with notes of things we want to discuss. I lead off, using the sandwich cookie approach—first something positive, then the concerns, and finish with something positive again.

I try to have specific and concrete suggestions for each area of concern, but first I ask the staff if they have ideas or suggestions. If they do, and the ideas are workable, we start from their thoughts to build a plan for continued improvement. Building on an employee's idea is more likely to succeed than imposing a thought I have had.

Using their ideas first, we document the areas of concern, then the proposed timetable for improvement. Excellence is our goal, and we chart the map to get us there. Perfection is not the goal.

Using the key indicators of what we want from staff to direct our conversation is important for me, since it keeps the important matters ahead of the unimportant issues. We have had better success with this method of formal evaluation, in conjunction with the daily comments and evaluations, than with other processes.

Conclusion

Our experience has been that by adopting regular evaluations, we have been more successful in meeting our needs and expectations of continually improving the performance of the staff, and consequently our entire office. It has helped build better communication with the staff, letting them know we care about improvements in their skills; these skills are important to our clients getting the best possible legal service from our office. Using the Jim Collins standard, we think that our staff is on the right bus, and in the right seat.

The evaluation forms currently being used in our office are appended to this chapter. They probably are not the ones we will be using in a couple of years. Good luck.

Peterson & Waggoner, LLP
Employee Self-Evaluation

Employee:______________________ Job title: ______________________

Supervising Attorney: ____________________ Employment Date: ______

Please mark the appropriate box with an "X" then comment in regard to the box that was marked.

1. KNOWLEDGE

Knowledge of job: Familiarity with the various procedures of the workload.

Unsatisfactory	Marginal	Satisfactory	Good	Excellent
Inadequate. Relies on others.	Insufficient knowledge of some phases of the job.	Adequate knowledge of particular job.	Thorough knowledge of of all phases of work.	Exceptional mastery of of all phases of work.
Comment				

2. QUANTITY OF WORK

A. Use of time: Appraise productive application of time. Does the employee stick to the job and/or ask for additional work when not busy?

Unsatisfactory	Marginal	Satisfactory	Good	Excellent
Talks or is away from job a lot. Could accomplish much more in same time.	Spends more time away than necessary. Could accomplish more	Only spends reasonable amount of time away from job.	Steady worker. Seldom away from job. Seeks additional work	Energetic. Spends no time away from job unnecessarily.
Comment				

B. **Amount:** Measure against the normal of standard amount expected on this job.

Unsatisfactory	Marginal	Satisfactory	Good	Excellent
Unable to do standard amount.	Frequently does less than standard amount.	Does standard amount.	Production will average more than standard amount.	Regularly produces more than average.
Comment				

3. QUALITY OF WORK

A. **Accuracy:** General accuracy and carefulness of work.

Unsatisfactory	Marginal	Satisfactory	Good	Excellent
Very careless. Often makes mistakes.	Work usually passable, some errors, should do better.	Meets standards with occasional errors.	Good work, few errors.	Very careful, errors rare.
Comment				

B. **Completeness:** How thoroughly are details attended to?

Unsatisfactory	Marginal	Satisfactory	Good	Excellent
Work usually done in a careless manner.	Some details of work often need correction should be improved.	Shows interest in doing a good job. Occasionally needs direction.	Usually is thorough, attends to details satisfactorily.	Very thorough in attention to details.
Comment				

C. **Initiative:** How much does employee anticipate needs of attorney, client or office?

Unsatisfactory	Marginal	Satisfactory	Good	Excellent
Has to be told what to do. Not interested in more work or projects.	Seldom takes initiative alone. Rarely makes suggestions.	Attentive to normal situations but wants help if at all out of the ordinary.	Suggests improvements Attempts to learn related jobs.	Constantly developing and improving skills and business relationship.
Comment				

4. CLIENT RELATIONS SKILLS

Concern: How concerned is the employee with servicing client needs?

Unsatisfactory	Marginal	Satisfactory	Good	Excellent
Does not try and apparently does not care.	Offers little useful response to clients.	Courteous and helpful.	Tries to help and assist clients.	Energetically assists clients and develops a business relationship.
Comment				

5. INTERPERSONAL RELATIONS

A. **Attitude toward others:** How does employee get along with people, including but not limited to supervisor and fellow employees?

Unsatisfactory	Marginal	Satisfactory	Good	Excellent
Quarrelsome, jealous, fault finding, uncooperative	Sometimes tactless and inconsiderate. to clients. understanding.	Normally makes a satisfactory impression.	Generally cooperative, friendly, understanding and helpful.	Very tactful and considerate Well liked, accepts adversity gracefully.
Comment				

B. Communication Skills: How are the employee's skills in participating as a eam player and working cooperatively with clients and accepting advice and counseling from supervisor?

Unsatisfactory	Marginal	Satisfactory	Good	Excellent
Does not try and apparently does not care.	Offers little useful response to the team.	Courteous and helpful.	Tries to help and assist other team. members	Energetically offers assistance to the team.
Comment				

6. ADAPTABILITY

A. **Initiative:** Does employee have the desire or ability to initiate work or ideas?

Unsatisfactory	Marginal	Satisfactory	Good	Excellent
Has to be told what to do. Not interested in more work or new jobs.	Seldom takes action alone. Rarely makes suggestions.	Handles normal situations well but wants help if at all out of the ordinary.	Suggests improvements Attempts to learn all related jobs.	Constantly developing and improving work methods.
Comment				

B. **Personal adjustment:** Appraise the ease with which personal adjustment is made to any change in job methods, personnel, supervisors, or surroundings.

Unsatisfactory	Marginal	Satisfactory	Good	Excellent
Any changes are opposed and usually cause trouble.	Somewhat resentful of change Cannot always see why necessary.	Makes normal adjustment to changes.	Adjusts willingly to changes.	Changes do not disturb at all. Helps with changes.
Comment				

7. ATTENDANCE AND PUNCTUALITY

Promptness: How much can you depend on the employee to be punctual and ready to begin the day?

Unsatisfactory	Marginal	Satisfactory	Good
Cannot be relied upon, must be watched continuously.	Needs frequent monitoring	Dependable, seldom needs supervision. adjustment	Always on time. Can be relied upon. No need to monitor.
Comment			

8. RELIABILITY

Dependability: How much can you depend on employee to complete work or projects on time?

Unsatisfactory	Marginal	Satisfactory	Good	Excellent
Cannot be relied upon at all, needs to be monitored continually.	Needs frequent monitoring.	Dependable with normal supervision.	Can be counted on, may require occasional spot check.	Deserves utmost confidence. No need to monitor Work done on time.
Comment				

9. If the employee is not performing all duties and responsibilities satisfactorily, please list and discuss improvement methods.

10. If particular objectives were set for in the past year, explain what they were and the results of these efforts.

11. What objectives are being set for the coming year?

12. General comments (i.e. strengths, weakness, methods to improve, etc.)

13. Overall performance:

Unsatisfactory	Marginal	Satisfactory	Good	Excellent
Major job responsibilities were not met, performance improvements. must be met in order to continue employment.	Met some of the expectation for the job, but performance improvements are still needed.	Met all the expectations of the job.	Exceeded many of the expectations of the job. Met and exceeded objectives in most areas.	Exceeded major expectations of the job. Consistently met and exceeded objectives in all areas.
Comment				

Employee comments:

Employee signature: ________________________________ Date: _____

Supervisor signature:________________________________ Date: _____

Peterson & Waggoner, LLP
Employee Evaluation

Employee:______________________ Job title: ______________________

Supervising Attorney: ____________________ Employment Date: ______

Current Wage: ____________ Number of days absent: ____

Please mark the appropriate box with an "X" then comment in regard to the box that was marked.

1. KNOWLEDGE
Knowledge of job: Familiarity with the various procedures of the workload.

Unsatisfactory	Marginal	Satisfactory	Good	Excellent
Inadequate. Relies on others.	Insufficient knowledge of some phases of the job.	Adequate knowledge of particular job.	Thorough knowledge of of all phases of work.	Exceptional mastery of of all phases of work.
Comment				

2. QUANTITY OF WORK
A. Use of time: Appraise productive application of time. Does the employee stick to the job and/or ask for additional work when not busy?

Unsatisfactory	Marginal	Satisfactory	Good	Excellent
Talks or is away from job a lot. Could accomplish much more in same time.	Spends more time away than necessary. Could accomplish more	Only spends reasonable amount of time away from job.	Steady worker. Seldom away from job. Seeks additional work	Energetic. Spends no time away from job unnecessarily.
Comment				

B. **Amount:** Measure against the normal of standard amount expected on this job.

Unsatisfactory	Marginal	Satisfactory	Good	Excellent
Unable to do standard amount.	Frequently does less than standard amount.	Does standard amount.	Production will average more than standard amount.	Regularly produces more than average.
Comment				

3. QUALITY OF WORK

A. **Accuracy:** General accuracy and carefulness of work.

Unsatisfactory	Marginal	Satisfactory	Good	Excellent
Very careless. Often makes mistakes.	Work usually passable, some errors, should do better.	Meets standards with occasional errors.	Good work, few errors.	Very careful, errors rare.
Comment				

B. **Completeness:** How thoroughly are details attended to?

Unsatisfactory	Marginal	Satisfactory	Good	Excellent
Work usually done in a careless manner.	Some details of work often need correction should be improved.	Shows interest in doing a good job. Occasionally needs direction.	Usually is thorough, attends to details satisfactorily.	Very thorough in attention to details.
Comment				

C. **Initiative:** How much does employee anticipate needs of attorney, client or office?

Unsatisfactory	Marginal	Satisfactory	Good	Excellent
Has to be told what to do. Not interested in more work or projects.	Seldom takes initiative alone. Rarely makes suggestions.	Attentive to normal situations but wants help if at all out of the ordinary.	Suggests improvements Attempts to learn related jobs.	Constantly developing and improving skills and business relationship.
Comment				

4. CLIENT RELATIONS SKILLS

Concern: How concerned is the employee with servicing client needs?

Unsatisfactory	Marginal	Satisfactory	Good	Excellent
Does not try and apparently does not care.	Offers little useful response to clients.	Courteous and helpful.	Tries to help and assist clients.	Energetically assists clients and develops a business relationship.
Comment				

5. INTERPERSONAL RELATIONS

A. **Attitude toward others:** How does employee get along with people, including but not limited to supervisor and fellow employees?

Unsatisfactory	Marginal	Satisfactory	Good	Excellent
Quarrelsome, jealous, fault finding, uncooperative	Sometimes tactless and inconsiderate. to clients. understanding.	Normally makes a satisfactory impression.	Generally cooperative, friendly, understanding and helpful.	Very tactful and considerate Well liked, accepts adversity gracefully.
Comment				

B. Communication Skills: How are the employee's skills in participating as a eam player and working cooperatively with clients and accepting advice and counseling from supervisor?

Unsatisfactory	Marginal	Satisfactory	Good	Excellent
Does not try and apparently does not care.	Offers little useful response to the team.	Courteous and helpful.	Tries to help and assist other team. members	Energetically offers assistance to the team.
Comment				

6. ADAPTABILITY

A. **Initiative:** Does employee have the desire or ability to initiate work or ideas?

Unsatisfactory	Marginal	Satisfactory	Good	Excellent
Has to be told what to do. Not interested in more work or new jobs.	Seldom takes action alone. Rarely makes suggestions.	Handles normal situations well but wants help if at all out of the ordinary.	Suggests improvements Attempts to learn all related jobs.	Constantly developing and improving work methods.
Comment				

B. **Personal adjustment:** Appraise the ease with which personal adjustment is made to any change in job methods, personnel, supervisors, or surroundings.

Unsatisfactory	Marginal	Satisfactory	Good	Excellent
Any changes are opposed and usually cause trouble.	Somewhat resentful of change Cannot always see why necessary.	Makes normal adjustment to changes.	Adjusts willingly to changes.	Changes do not disturb at all. Helps with changes.
Comment				

7. ATTENDANCE AND PUNCTUALITY

Promptness: How much can you depend on the employee to be punctual and ready to begin the day?

Unsatisfactory	Marginal	Satisfactory	Good
Cannot be relied upon, must be watched continuously.	Needs frequent monitoring	Dependable, seldom needs supervision. adjustment	Always on time. Can be relied upon. No need to monitor.
Comment			

8. RELIABILITY

Dependability: How much can you depend on employee to complete work or projects on time?

Unsatisfactory	Marginal	Satisfactory	Good	Excellent
Cannot be relied upon at all, needs to be monitored continually.	Needs frequent monitoring.	Dependable with normal supervision.	Can be counted on, may require occasional spot check.	Deserves utmost confidence. No need to monitor Work done on time.
Comment				

9. If the employee is not performing all duties and responsibilities satisfactorily, please list and discuss improvement methods.

10. If particular objectives were set for in the past year, explain what they were and the results of these efforts.

11. What objectives are being set for the coming year?

12. General comments (i.e. strengths, weakness, methods to improve, etc.)

13. Overall performance:

Unsatisfactory	Marginal	Satisfactory	Good	Excellent
Major job responsibilities were not met, performance improvements. must be met in order to continue employment.	Met some of the expectation for the job, but performance improvements are still needed.	Met all the expectations of the job.	Exceeded many of the expectations of the job. Met and exceeded objectives in most areas.	Exceeded major expectations of the job. Consistently met and exceeded objectives in all areas.
Comment				

Employee comments:

Employee signature: ______________________________ Date: _____

Supervisor signature:______________________________ Date: _____

Workplace Security for Solo and Small Firm Staff

19

by David Zachary Kaufman

What? Me Worry?

Actually, yes. You should worry about your workplace security. Statistics don't seem to be available for violent incidents in lawyers' offices, but anecdotally a large number of violent events seem to be occurring. In recent years we've all read about judges being shot by irate litigants, law firms (both large and small) being invaded by upset clients, and lawyers shooting other lawyers.

What, then, is the threat? Well, astonishingly enough, all the above are not the only problem. In fact, if law firms are like other offices, the greatest threat of violence in the office comes from within: The biggest threat to you and your staff are your significant life partners. How could this be? Simply put, if a client or opponent is upset with your firm, they almost always give some sort of warning and, if you follow the procedures below, you will be able to respond appropriately. But a significant life partner, on the other hand, is just that. So it's almost inconceivable that the partner would become violent or bring violence to the workplace no matter how abusive outside of work. (Anyone who has ever worked with domestic abuse knows how frequently the abused partner is in denial.)

What Are You Going to Do about It?

Well, that's what this chapter is all about. This chapter will give you some basic ideas of what you need to do to protect yourself, your staff, and your business from violence and the threat of violence.

The first thing you, the business owner, have to do is make a decision: Do you want to protect yourself, your staff, and your business? If so, good! To do this, however, you will have to do a few things—not necessarily expensive things. Most important, you must anticipate potential problems and develop plans to deal with them. These problems will come from clients, opponents, opposing counsel, staff, and your own personal life. The solutions will come from how you respond.

Let's Start with the Office

When you design your office, there are things you can do that will dramatically increase office security. There are also office procedures you can insist upon that will have the same effect.

Security Starts Outside the Office

If you own the office building, most local police will come out and give advice on how to secure the building and any associated parking lot. As far as I know, this service is free. Take advantage of it. If you are renting, ask the owner what he or she is doing about security. Any good landlord wants tenants to be safe. Ask the police to examine the office space you propose to rent and make suggestions.

When you first arrive at the building, check the parking lot for good lighting and overgrown shrubbery. Is there a clear, well-lighted path to the front door? How about the area around the door? Is it clear or overgrown? Can people hide in the shadows close to the door? If there is an intercom system, does it actually work?

When you go inside, check to see if the restroom doors lock. They should. If they do, who has the keys? Sadly, restrooms are favorite sites for attacks, as the patrons are usually distracted. Check that the stairways are well-lit. While you are doing that, don't forget to check the stairway's doors, especially the doors to the outside. If the exit doors don't lock, there is a problem that should be fixed.

Office Design

An Inner Door Should Separate the Work Area from Reception.

When violence intrudes into the office, it usually comes swiftly. The front door swings open and everything starts. That's why every office should have a locking inner door separating the reception area from the general workspace. Depending on they exact type of law you practice (e.g., collections, divorce, bankruptcy, criminal, commercial, etc.), you will have to decide where your receptionist should be and, if you can afford the space, where your conference room should be.

A lot depends on you, your budget, and how consumer-friendly you wish to appear. At a minimum, your receptionist should have a place to hide behind the desk that is somewhat secure. (You can install a sheet of Kevlar bulletproof material or the equivalent under the desk for a few hundred dollars at most.) If you can afford it, and you want the receptionist in front of the inner door, don't use just a desk for the receptionist; build a workspace that provides additional security. If you want the receptionist behind the inner door, use a clear, unbreakable polymer (available in all thicknesses and strengths and for various prices) so he or she can see and be seen without being too vulnerable. Anyone who visits the firm should be announced by the receptionist, and only when their visit is confirmed should they be buzzed in. This procedure is critically important and will be discussed in more detail below.

The Inner Door Should Be Strong and Have an Alarm.

If you do not have a receptionist but have a reception area, you should still have the inner door. Get a chime at the front door that rings whenever the door is opened. It will help keep track of people coming in and going out. They aren't expensive and are readily available. In this case, the design of the inner door should be different if you don't have a receptionist—put in a peephole or something similar so you can see who is there and examine their demeanor. As an alternative to a peephole, consider one of the new cheap digital cameras that will feed directly into your computer. That way, if the cameras are correctly mounted, you can check instantly when you hear something and are working late or expecting a visitor. Then, if all is well, you can let them in. If you don't have a reception area, you still have an alternative to just letting people walk in: Ask visitors to buzz for permission to enter. Then either use a peephole in your front door or use one of the digital feed cameras and follow the same procedures as if there is a reception area but no receptionist.

The locking inner door should be both key-operated and controlled by a buzzer at the receptionist's desk. The buzzer should be mounted under the desktop, not on top. Why? Because you should have a panic switch mounted under the desk too—on the opposite side. (Left side for buzzer, right side for panic switch.) The locking inner door should not be hollow, as most inner doors are. It should be a solid wood door opening toward the workplace side of the wall, hiding the hinges. When the door is installed, the locks and hinges should be securely fastened to the door frame with at least 3-inch screws.

If you cannot afford a panic system, a cell phone with speed-dial "9" set to "911" can be a reasonable substitute.

Your Conference Room Should Be Off the Reception Area.

If you can afford the space, have your conference room off the reception area rather than in the back. This will enhance security, protect your secrets and confidences, and (possibly) reduce overhead.

The Office Should Have a Back Door.

If it is at all possible, every office should have a back-door exit that takes people out of the office without going through the main entrance. If a back door it is not possible, the back working area should have a "panic room," which is reinforced with a solid door and other protections in which people can take refuge if necessary. The panic room can be your own office with a reinforced door with a heavy lock, designed to open inwards to conceal the hinges, and some other inexpensive items like a peephole.

Your Windows Should Be Protected.

All the windows and other means of entry, even the attic vents, should be secured and have an alarm if needed. Be sure to have your landlord trim the shrubbery away from both the doors and windows of the basement and first floor. If there are trees nearby, consider whether upper-floor windows can be reached from the nearby trees. If so, secure them as well. The methods of securing windows and doors can be very inexpensive—maybe as little as $5 per window or door.

Windows should also have curtains or blinds or some other treatment that can be closed so that people can look out but cannot be seen. Only recently in Las Vegas a judge was shot by a disappointed litigant through the window in his chambers. Apparently the judge was looking out his window, and the man shot the judge from another building. Fortunately, the judge lived and the man was caught. (It's frequently a man but not always, and you should never generalize.)

Your Personal Office.

As you personalize your office, keep security in mind. I recommend ensuring that the door is solid, not hollow, and that the locks are strong. You may wish to install a peephole. Alternatively, you could install the digital cameras and run their output into your computer so you can check what's going on. If your office has windows, any curtains or window treatments should be designed so you can look out but others cannot look in. This is especially true if you have a ground-floor office or one overlooked by other buildings or trees.

If you have a custom desk, or even a simple one from Office Depot or Staples, you can install a panic switch on the underside of the desk or on the floor. Some people put the switch beneath the slide-out drawer for their keyboard. What counts is that you can reach it easily and inconspicuously if something happens.

There is a school of thought that you should keep a weapon (handgun, Taser, Mace, etc.) available. If you are part of that school of thought, be sure to comply with the local laws. Weapons besides firearms are frequently regulated. I know that some cities, such as Washington, D.C., and New York City, have either outlawed or require licenses for Tasers, pepper spray, Mace, and similar weapons. Others do not. Check carefully, as the consequences of a mistake are grave. Before putting any weapon in your office, however, ask yourself a question: Are you willing to use it on another human being? If you are not sure, maybe you shouldn't have it. If you are sure, be sure to practice with it so you can use it effectively. Practice with Mace and pepper spray. Be sure you learn to hit what you are aiming at with the spray and to spray with, not into, the wind. You really don't want pepper spray blown back into your own face.

Get an Intruder Alarm.

Finally, your office should be equipped with an intruder alarm that also contains a panic function so help can be summoned whenever necessary. Not a burglar alarm, an *intruder* alarm. What's the difference? The intruder alarm can be set to go off even when you are in the office if someone gets past the reception area. There are many brands and companies offering this service, some better and some worse. It's impossible to generalize, as these companies vary tremendously by geographic region. But usually they are not too expensive.

Whatever service you get, be sure it includes a "panic switch." What is a panic switch, you ask? That's the button you press when someone bursts past reception and you need to signal the police for immediate help. A well-designed system will also alert the people in the back work area that there is an intruder so that they can either go out the back door or lock themselves into the panic room.

The panic switch should be mounted at the reception area (as described above) and under your desk. Be sure that the system you buy permits you to appear to be turning it off but signals that you are acting under duress. One thing: Be sure you teach your staff where the alarm is located and how to use it. Amazingly enough, many people don't do that and then wonder why their staff didn't sound the alarm.

Office Procedures

Every office should have a handbook of office procedures. Most of the handbooks I have reviewed talk about emergencies, e-mail policy, and similar things. Security issues should also be discussed in the handbook, and the requirements should be clear. Many, but not all, the issues that should be in the handbook are described below.

Threats Must Be Reported.

Staff should be told that it is an absolute rule that all threats, regardless of whether or not the staff believes the threat is credible, must be reported to you personally. If you are not available, they must be reported to your office manager. Staff also must be told that "all threats" means *all threats*, including threats from present or former significant life partners and other members of their extended relationships. Staff should be told that you will maintain confidentiality as much as possible, but the safety of staff and the firm must come first.

Clients Must Have an Appointment.

It should be basic: If you don't have an appointment, you don't get in. This is particularly true of other parties and opposing counsel. It should apply to clients and friends, too, but I do understand that it could be a problem. Regardless of who is visiting, the receptionist must check with the host before buzzing visitors into the work area. This is absolutely critical—significant life partners and enraged clients are most often violent, closely followed by the other party and opposing counsel. The receptionist should always check the computer for a "flag" while notifying the host that a visitor has arrived.

In my practice I do not take "walk-ins," but other practices do. So this principle need not apply to new clients. (After all, how angry can they be if they just met you?) To avoid pretextual visits, however, the receptionist should require visitors to properly identify themselves. Then the receptionist should run a quick check in the computer to see if there are flags requiring action. This can be done easily by asking the new client to fill out an intake form and show identification. Again, staff absolutely must get clearance before sending any new client back into the work area or even into the conference room.

No Information About You Is Ever Given Out.

On a related note, staff should never give out any information over the phone to anybody without checking with you or the affected person first. That includes your schedule, phone number, type of car, where you are going, when you will be back, or any other information. You simply don't want people to know when you or your staff are working late and might be alone in the office. You also don't want anyone to know when the office is empty; sabotage is always a possibility, as are various computer traps like key counters and viruses.

Similarly, don't follow a predictable pattern, especially in your visits to the bank. It may be hard to do if you have a litigation practice, but work on it. Frankly, any predictability makes it easier to find you, and it's hard not to be at least a little predictable. There was a recent case in the news where one lawyer shot another outside the courthouse. Why the courthouse? Because everyone knew where the lawyer would be that day.

Protect Your Technology.

There should be (and are) special classes to teach people how to safeguard their electronic data. Computers, cell phones, PDAs, etc., are so important to the practice of law now that I wonder how we functioned without them. It is because they are so important that data security is so important. The solution is simple and cheap: Use a password. Use a password on everything—PDAs, computers, thumb drives, key documents on the computer, etc. If you use a laptop, this is especially important.

If you think about how you can be tracked—how people can infer where you live, where you go, what behavior patterns you exhibit—it can make you shudder with fear. It certainly scares me. Others may differ, but I recommend using strong passwords based on phrases you and only you will recall. Also, experts in the field recommend changing your passwords regularly. I'll take their word for it, but it sure is inconvenient.

Something truly important that I must alert you to: Many times staff put their passwords on yellow stickers and put the stickers on their monitors. Or they put the passwords on note cards in the desk drawer. That should be forbidden. No excuses. It makes access to your system a joke.

Another absolutely forbidden action: leaving the workstation and not password-protecting the monitor. Imagine that! Then, when someone wants to get into your system, all that person has to do is move a mouse. Given the small size of digital cameras and thumb drives, to say nothing of access to the Internet, how much easier can you make it to hack into your system?

If You or Your Staff Have Been Threatened

In this chapter I assume that you or your staff have been threatened. The first question is simple: Is this threat serious? If you judge that it is merely hot air, then that ends the matter. But can you be sure the threat is not serious? Most of us cannot tell. So you go to the next step: figuring out if the threat is serious. You may need to consult the police or another expert. If the threat came from a current or former client, you have another problem: Is the threat a client confidence or secret? If you are not sure, or if you are sure but are not sure if you can disclose the confidence or secret under the circumstances, check with your local bar association practice management advisor. Check immediately—don't wait. Time could be of the essence.

It should go without saying that if you are being threatened by a client, you should fire the client immediately. I would also, as I fire the client, strongly advise the client of the problems inherent in carrying out the threat, including the obvious fact that people will know who did it.

First Steps

Immediately after the office receives notice of a credible threat, certain steps should be taken by either the lawyer or the office manager. The first thing to do is to notify all staff and the other lawyers that there might be a problem and ask them to be careful. If it is possible, given privacy and ethical concerns, tell people who to be alert for. Then call the police. After you have called the police, do the same with the building manager, janitorial staff, and your neighbors. Tell them what is going on and ask them to notify you and/or call the police if they see something suspicious. Where at all possible (given privacy and ethical concerns), be sure that you describe the person.

Having made these calls and taken advice (or while you are waiting for the bar advisor to call you back), be sure to document the threat. Include the person's name, address, Social Security number (if known), age or date of birth, phone numbers, etc. Do not forget to link that person to the case or cases.

If you cannot divulge the identity of the person who made the threat due to client confidentiality, I recommend that you put the documentation into an envelope, seal the envelope, and give it to a lawyer you know and trust with instructions to open the envelope only upon your death or serious injury.

Second Steps

If the threat was phoned in, notify the telephone company. Include the date and time and, if possible, the duration of the call. Sometimes they can help. If the threat comes by e-mail or fax, do the same. If you have a recording of a threatening message, be sure to preserve it for evidence.

Regardless of where the threat came from, and absent client confidentiality issues, call the police and file a formal complaint. Sometimes the police will resist, but you should insist. Then demand that the police arrest the person. They may or may not do that, but try. As part of the complaint, you should be sure to invoke (if your state has one) the law guaranteeing privacy and that criminalizes harassing and intimidating telephone calls, mail, faxes, e-mail, text messaging, FaceBook or MySpace posts, etc. If you have to, use the WayBackMachine (http://www.archive.org/web/web.php) to recover and preserve the evidence of these acts.

We're lawyers, so we know how to use the law. File for a temporary restraining order to keep the threatener away from you, your staff, and your firm. You may wish to demand that the person keep away from your home and family, too. It all depends on who is threatened. Then get an injunction extending the restraining order. Use the evidence you should have been collecting and preserving as described above.

When you do go to court about the restraining orders or about the underlying case, be sure to notify the bailiff and/or the local sheriff about your fears, the actions you have taken to protect yourself, and the restraining orders. Take copies of the orders with you when you go to court, and show them to anyone who asks. Ask that you be escorted to your car or wherever you need to go. Sometimes the bailiffs will cooperate or ask a nearby policeman or deputy to escort you.

General Precautions Are Good

After reporting the threat and getting the temporary restraining order, be sure to take extra precautions, and have your staff take extra precautions as well. Depending on how worried you are, you might wish to invest in some protective clothing. I know, I know. It sounds like I'm talking about dressing up like a SWAT team or something. But I'm not. Simple things work wonders. For example, did you know that they make attaché cases lined with Kevlar bulletproof material? These briefcases look just like any other case, hold papers, and are fully functional. They just weigh a little more than the usual. But if you hold it up in front of your body it acts like a shield against getting shot. Kevlar is amazing stuff! Equally amazing, these briefcases only cost about $1,200. That's not so much more than a lot of briefcases I see around the courthouse these days anyway.

Other than the courthouse, the one place everyone sooner or later returns to is their car. So be extra careful when you return to your car. There are many possible tips and tip sheets out there about driving your car or approaching your car, and most are decent. The key point that they all make is that "eternal vigilance is the price of liberty." It's true: You must be alert to your surroundings at all time. Only then can you be secure.

Conclusion

It doesn't have to cost a lot to be secure. But you do have to think about it and prepare. Good luck.

Part VI

Knowledge of Employment Law Never Hurts

Even in the lawyer's own office, employment law still applies. Do you know your rights and responsibilities as an employer?

Discrimination in the Solo and Small Firm

20

by Laura V. Farber

For the solo and small firm practitioner, there are both federal and state laws that deal with discrimination in the workplace. This chapter is intended to be a brief overview of the federal laws, a short discussion of state law examples, and a discussion of preventive steps that you, as a solo or small firm practitioner, can take to avoid being on the receiving end of a lawsuit from a current or former employee on the grounds of discrimination.

Overview of Federal Law Regarding Discrimination

An employer's principal obligations under federal law regarding discrimination are found in Title VII of the Civil Rights Act of 1964, the Americans with Disabilities Act of 1990 (ADA), the Equal Pay Act of 1963, and the Age Discrimination in Employment Act of 1967 (ADEA). The federal agency that is delegated responsibility to monitor compliance with these laws is the Equal Employment Opportunity Commission (EEOC). Although most states, if not all, have civil rights laws that duplicate the federal laws in many respects, usually these laws do not supersede one another. So, in order to be certain what the law requires and what a solo/small firm's employment obligations are, all applicable laws, both federal and the applicable laws in your state, need to be examined independently.

If you, as a solo or small firm practitioner, employ 15 or more employees, you are covered by Title VII and the ADA. Title VII prohibits employers who are covered by the law from employment discrimination on the grounds of race, color, sex, religion, national origin, or pregnancy-related conditions. The ADA prohibits discrimination against a qualified disabled individual regarding any term, condition, or privilege of employment. This also covers hiring, discharge, compensation, promotion, and training. Specifically, the ADA protects individuals with mental or physical disabilities. Title VII is not strictly limited to protecting an employee since discrimination is prohibited against any individual, which could include a partner, independent contractor, or a successor.

The Equal Pay Act is under the Fair Labor Standards Act (FLSA) Section 6(b). If you are covered by the FLSA, you are subject to the Equal Pay Act. As a small-firm practitioner, you are covered by the FLSA if your annual gross sales or business (exclusive of retail sales tax) is at least $500,000 and you have two or more employees engaged in either interstate commerce or the production of goods through interstate commerce or handling, selling, or otherwise working on goods or materials that are produced for interstate commerce. The Equal Pay Act requires an employer to pay equal pay for similar work requiring equal skill, effort and responsibility.

If you have 20 or more employees, you are covered by the ADEA. The ADEA prevents discrimination against individuals who are at least 40 or older. The ADEA covers discrimination regarding hiring, firing, compensation, terms, conditions, and privileges of employment.

Sex Discrimination in the Workplace

Sex discrimination is covered by Title VII under federal law as well as federal common law. The EEOC has issued sex discrimination guidelines regarding their enforcement positions. Interestingly, federal courts have concluded that discrimination on the basis of sexual orientation is not included in the ban against discrimination on the basis of sex contained in Title VII. This particular form of discrimination is also not covered by the ADA. However, the EEOC and at least one decision of the Ninth Circuit have held that same sex harassment violates Title VII.

Claims of sexual harassment are commonly asserted against employers under Title VII and applicable state statutes. Both state and federal laws recognize two types of sexual harassment claims, quid pro quo claims and hostile work environment claims. A quid pro quo harassment claim is essentially when an unwelcomed request for a sexual favor or a sexual advance is a condition of employment, a promotion, or the receipt of some other employment benefit. A hostile work environment claim occurs where there is unwelcome physical, verbal or visual conduct that is sexual and interferes with the work environment such that an individual cannot perform their work because they are intimidated, or the work environment is too hostile or too offensive. The EEOC has its rules dealing with unlawful sex discrimination and specifically with sexual harassment under Title VII. The rules are a guide in interpreting what kind of conduct constitutes sexual harassment.

EEOC Enforcement of Federal Laws

If a current or former employee chooses to pursue a federal claim for discrimination under Title VII, the ADEA, or ADA, he or she must file a complaint with the EEOC to exhaust administrative remedies. When such a complaint is filed, the EEOC usually contacts the employer to discuss the allegation, especially when a right to sue letter is not immediately requested. In other words, many claimants may choose to use the EEOC to pursue the actual claim, instead of hiring an attorney to do so. If the EEOC finds, through its response from the employer and its own investigation, that there could be liability, the EEOC, with the complainant's consent, will pursue the claim against the employer. If, however, a current or former employee retains an attorney with interest in pursuing a lawsuit, and an immediate request for a right to sue letter is made, the EEOC simply processes the complaint and immediately closes its file and issues a right to sue letter. If you receive any kind of a complaint or inquiry from the EEOC, it is imperative that you promptly and thoroughly respond to the EEOC's request. If you do so, and the EEOC is pursuing a thorough investigation, many times, if you are able to persuade the EEOC that the claim has no validity, the EEOC will close the file and make a finding that there was no probable cause to pursue the claim.

When the EEOC receives a charge against an employer, it is required to notify the employer or the "respondent" within 10 days after the charges are filed. The charge has to set forth the date, time, place, and circumstances of the alleged unlawful practice. The EEOC is also required to make its finding, if it is pursuing an investigation as far as practicable, within one 120 days of the date the charge is filed or, if later, the date the EEOC is required to take action regarding the charge. Also, the EEOC has a work-sharing agreement with many states that also have their own administrative agency. State law claims can be pursued, and under the work-sharing agreement, when an employee or former employee files a charge with the state agency, it is deemed filed with both agencies and vice-versa.

Keep in mind, however, that if you do not employ 15 or more employees in your workplace, Title VII will not factor in a sexual harassment or other form of discrimination claim. It is for these reasons that a smaller employer (an employer with less than 15 employees), is generally not subject to the federal laws that have just been briefly described in this overview.

It is also important to note however, that employers with fewer than fifteen employees who are ordinarily exempt from Title VII, are subject to the Immigration Reform Control Act of 1986 (IRCA) citizenship and natural origin discrimination rules, provided that they have at least four employees.

State Laws Prohibiting Discrimination

Although a discussion of state laws is well beyond what a general and national chapter can cover, since the author is from California, that state will be used as an example of both state statutory schemes and common-law claims that could apply to a solo and small firm practitioner, possibly rendering the practitioner liable for claims of discrimination.

Generally, many states have their own civil rights laws consisting of statutory and, in many cases, common-law claims. In California, virtually all California employers with five or more employees are covered by the California Fair Employment and Housing Act (FEHA). The employers who are exempt from FEHA coverage are businesses and enterprises that do not regularly employ five or more persons on a full-time or part-time basis. However, the FEHA prohibitions that pertain to unlawful harassment apply to any person or business that regularly employs one or more persons, including a person who is acting as the employer's agent. Accordingly, in California, the solo or small firm practitioner who regularly employs five or more persons on a full time or part time basis, will be covered by the provisions of the FEHA statute, and solo and small firm practitioners that employ one or more persons will be covered by the prohibitions against unlawful harassment. Further, plaintiffs can pursue common-law causes of action such as torts for wrongful termination, constructive discharge, discrimination on protected grounds, such as those set forth in Title VII, and in the case of California, sexual orientation, marital status, medical condition, genetic characteristics, and gender identity. Accordingly, it is imperative to have a familiarity with your respective state's civil rights statutory scheme, if any, and common-law causes of action, which in many instances exist to cover all employers regardless of size.

Many state agencies have set forth sex discrimination guidelines. In many states, it is a prerequisite to exhaust administrative remedies prior to filing a lawsuit. Once again, in the case of California, the Department of Fair Employment and Housing (DFEH) is the agency that enforces the FEHA law and the agency where an employee or former employee will commence an administrative charge with any allegations of discrimination. Much like the EEOC, the DFEH will either open a file and investigate the claim or immediately issue a right to sue letter if the employee or former employee is interested in pursuing claims in court. Since many states have a work-sharing arrangement with their agencies and the EEOC, if an employee or former employee chooses to mix state and federal law claims in a lawsuit, it is not necessary to file two separate administrative charges and obtain two separate right to sue letters to pursue a claim in either federal or state court.

State Law Sexual Harassment Claims

The most common claim that will confront an employer, including solo and small firm lawyers, is that of sexual or other forms of harassment. Sexual harassment constitutes one of the most common types of claims filed against employers under Title VII and state statutes. Sexual harassment is considered a form of unlawful sex discrimination under Title VII and most state statutes. Both the EEOC and many state agencies have issued rules that recognize sexual harassment as an unlawful form of sex discrimination. Rules broadly reference the type of conduct that constitutes sexual harassment. Employers can be held responsible for inappropriate conduct committed by their managers, supervisors, and many times by non-supervisory employees. In some states, customers, vendors, and clients who engage in inappropriate conduct toward an employee, can also create liability for an employer. It is also important to recognize that the sexual harassment does not need to occur during working hours, or at the work place, in order to constitute an actionable claim.

Another form of discrimination that arises out of sexual harassment claims is retaliation for complaining about sexual harassment, either internally or by pursuing a charge with either the EEOC or a state agency. An employee or former employee can also pursue attorneys' fees in sexual harassment cases. Additionally, some states will also find the individual who is found to have engaged in inappropriate sexual harassment personally liable. These claims are not limited to statutory theories, but can also be the subject of tort claims such as wrongful discharge, infliction of emotional distress, assault, battery, constructive discharge, and defamation.

Harassment Policies

It is for these reasons that it is prudent for all solo and small firm employers to have sexual harassment and other forms of harassment policy in place with procedures that can be used to address the issues that frequently arise in any size and type of work environment.

Federal law and most state law focus on measures taken by an employer to prevent harassment. Further, preventive measures undertaken pursuant to a harassment policy can protect an employer from the adverse consequences of harassment, and also discourage inappropriate behavior. Policies are also helpful in preventing litigation.

It is very helpful for employers of all sizes, including solo and small firm practitioners, to have in place measures and policies that will sensitize employees regarding the prohibition against sexual harassment and other unlawful forms of harassment. It is important to have a written policy that is clearly communicated and provided to all employees, especially supervisors. The policy should be simply written; should address all forms of unlawful harassment prohibited by federal and/or state laws; should provide for a complaint procedure that does not require an employee to complain directly to his or her supervisor; and should require the prompt investigation of any complaint. A policy also should explicitly state that there will be no retaliation or reprisal for pursuing a complaint under the policy.

Another benefit of having a written policy in place is in defending a claim of hostile work environment as a form of harassment. Although such a policy does not necessarily constitute a complete defense to all of these types of claims, it may serve various useful purposes, including limiting a damages claim and showing that the policy was in place and perhaps an employee did not choose to follow it. Some of the other benefits of having a written policy include that it allows the employer to promptly respond to and investigate a claim of harassment; enables the employer to take immediate and corrective action where appropriate pursuant to a complaint; and helps the employer publicize the policy so that all employees in the workplace are aware of it. Also, a policy ensures that all managers and/or supervisors will support and follow the policy, and perhaps prevent an award of punitive damages when the trier of fact considers that an employer has a policy in place. A policy can also show that an employer has conducted enforcement and educated its employees in good faith against harassment. Depending on the nature of the complaint, an employer can choose to provide corrective action, such as transferring an employee to a different work area or space or having the employee work on items that do not involve interaction with the alleged harasser. The employer can also discipline the alleged harasser and, depending on the nature of the harassment, consider termination of the alleged harasser as well as any other steps that are reasonably calculated to eliminate harassment.

It is important to note that harassment can be based on characteristics that are protected by both federal and state law, including race, religion, color, age, disability, national origin, and, of course, sex. Also, depending on the state, harassment laws may include harassment on the basis of sexual orientation, marital status, citizenship, or medical condition.

Many states will require he posting of policy and/or state agency and information sheets so that an employee is aware of his or her rights, not only with respect to internal policies of the employer, but also with respect to pursuing statutory and other claims, covered under either federal law or state law. Although it is certainly not required, it may be helpful, depending on how many supervisors the solo or small firm practitioner, to provide some training for those supervisors on harassment.

It is also helpful to request that all employees sign a notice of acknowledgment and receipt of the written policy so that at some later time, should a claim or complaint of harassment arise, the employee cannot argue or state that he or she did not receive the policy, know of its existence, or follow it. It is helpful to document both the investigation of any claims and communications relating to a claim of harassment. An employer can ask an independent outside human resources consultant or office manager to conduct an investigation and collect documentation. Also, any discipline that is needed with respect to an employee who has engaged in inappropriate harassment should be fully documented. Further, in many states, harassment is found to be a basis of liability if it is initiated by a customer and/or vendor against an employee and an investigation needs to take place to the extent it is possible, as well as efforts by you and/or your office manager to deal with the conduct.

The damages that can be assessed against an employer in a harassment claim can be substantial. They include emotional distress damages and punitive damages. In a case of harassment based on a discrimination argument, remedies can include back pay and lost benefits. Further, in many instances, both under Title VII and in many states, individuals can be personally liable for unlawful discrimination or harassment. However, under Title VII, an individual cannot be personally liable for creating a hostile environment.

Additionally, you as a solo or small firm practitioner, should remain aware of the highly sensitive nature of a harassment complaint and/or investigation, and keep in mind issues relating to confidentiality. Since these are usually claims that deal with the reputation or character of an employee, employment issues, and/or opportunities, promotions, etc., the greatest extent of confidentiality should be observed.

With respect to claims of constructive discharge and retaliation, the EEOC may find a constructive discharge even where an employee's resignation was not forced by an employer or an employer did not specifically intend for this to occur. The EEOC tends to focus on whether the employer has an effective internal grievance procedure. To prove a constructive discharge claim, there need to be working conditions that are so intolerable that a reasonable person in a similar situation would have no choice but to leave his or her position.

The U.S. Supreme Court has held that an employer can assert, as a defense to a constructive discharge claim, that it has an effective sexual harassment policy for the resolution of and reporting of complaints of sexual harassment and that the employee has unreasonably failed to avail himself or herself of that preventive or remedial policy. The affirmative defense is not available if the employee quits in response to an employer-sanctioned adverse action—demoting an employee or otherwise changing the employee's employment status.

Also, with respect to claims of harassment and retaliation, the U.S. Supreme Court has held that "simple teasing, offhand comments, and isolated incidents (unless extremely serious) will not amount to discriminatory changes in the terms and conditions of employment." This is in the context of retaliation. In order to prove a claim of retaliation, discriminatory changes in the terms and conditions of employment need to be shown.

In any event, it is helpful to put together an anti-harassment policy even for a solo and small firm practitioner that may only have common law liability, so that it will foster a more productive work environment that will prevent harassment from occurring and will engender loyalty and longevity, as well as high morale throughout the work environment.

Employment Law in the Solo and Small Firm

21

by Jennifer J. Ator

When it has employees, a business is required to follow both federal and state laws. Solo and small firms must comply with these laws and probably should be models for other professions. This chapter will discuss the federal laws and general categories of state laws that apply to solo and small-firm practitioners.

The first half of this chapter will analyze the laws that apply to small businesses, including the wage and hour laws. The second half of the chapter will discuss discrimination laws and how to avoid being on the receiving end of a discrimination or sexual harassment lawsuit from an employee.

General Federal Laws Governing Employers' Responsibilities

Solo and small-firm practitioners are required to comply with the federal and state laws governing employees. These laws include reporting requirements, insurance requirements, and protection of employees in the workplace.

Income Tax Withholding and Reporting

The Internal Revenue Service requires employers, upon hiring an employee, to complete a W-4 form. The form tells the employer how many withholding allowances to use when deducting federal income tax from an employee's pay. Generally, employers are required quarterly to file IRS Form 941, Employer's Quarterly Federal Tax Return, and annually to file IRS Form 940, Employer's Annual Federal Tax Return; Form W-2, Wage and Tax Statement; and Form W-3, Transmittal of Income and Tax Statements. A thorough explanation of an employer's requirements is found in Publication 15, *Employer's Tax Guide*, and Publication 15-A, *Employer's Supplemental Tax Guide*. All of these forms are found on the IRS Web site at www.irs.gov.

Immigration Eligibility Verification Requirements

Upon hiring an employee, an employer is also required to obtain employment eligibility verification. The Immigration Reform and Control Act made employers responsible for the verification of employment eligibility for all employees hired to work in the United States. The employer is required to maintain the I-9 form in its own files for all current employees, and for former employees the employer must maintain the form for either three years after the date of hire or one year after the date of termination, whichever occurs first. The I-9 forms must be stored in a place where inspection can be provided within three days. For large employers, I-9 forms are usually stored together, but for smaller employers, I-9 forms are often maintained in the employee's file. The penalty for failing to obtain and maintain the I-9 form ranges from $100 to $1,100 per employee. The I-9 form and employer information bulletins related to the I-9 form can be found at http://www.uscis.gov.

Worker's Compensation Insurance Requirements

Nearly every state makes worker's compensation insurance compulsory for private employers. These laws are state-specific but sometimes have a minimum number of employees (e.g., you might be exempt if you have fewer than three employees). Sometimes states do not require worker's compensation for certain types of workers, (e.g., office workers are not always required to be covered). But the exemptions are the rare exception, not the rule. Your commercial insurance carrier can usually provide you with worker's compensation insurance or provide a contact to ensure you are adequately covered under the law.

The federal government has also enacted the Occupational Safety & Health Act of 1970. While the act does not have specific requirements for office workers, it does apply to the office environment, and it has a general duty clause that requires employers to "furnish to each of his employees employment and a place of employment which are free from recognized hazards that are causing or likely to cause death or serious physical harm to his employees." Health and safety issues include insuring proper training and maintenance for equipment (including copiers and computers); maintaining building and grounds; ensuring housekeeping; providing adequate lighting, heating, and ventilation; and posting first aid information and evacuation plans for your office. The penalties that may be assessed by the federal government range from $5,000 to not more than $70,000 for each violation of the act. Twenty-four states have adopted state standards and policies, which should also be reviewed for compliance.

The U.S. Department of Labor has a small business handbook, which was specifically prepared to help small business employers meet the legal requirements imposed by the act. The handbook can be found at: http://www.osha.gov/Publications/smallbusiness/small-business.pdf.

Military Service and Your Employees

The Uniformed Services Employment and Reemployment Rights Act provides protection to employees who voluntarily or involuntarily undertake military service. As an employer, you are required to reemploy the service personnel to their civilian job if the employee 1) ensures you receive advance written or verbal notice of the service; 2) has five years or less of cumulative service in the uniformed services *while* with your firm; and 3) returns to work in a timely manner after conclusion of the service.

The employer must restore the employee to the job and benefits the employee would have attained if the employee had not been absent due to military service or, in some cases, to a comparable job. The Defense Department organization Employer Support of the Guard and Reserve has prepared an employer resource guide that answers specific questions related to the civilian reemployment of military personnel called to active duty. The resource guide can be found at http://www.esgr.org/files/toolkit/ESGR_HR_Guide_Final.pdf.

Unemployment Compensation

Generally, the federal and state unemployment programs require that states maintain a program to provide benefits to employees who are unemployed through no fault of their own (as determined by the state law). Each state administers its own program, but in the majority of the states, benefit funding is provided through a tax imposed on employers. Generally, as an employer, you are required to report and pay both federal and state payroll taxes for each of your employees if you pay wages to employees totaling $1,500, or more in any quarter of a calendar year or you have at least one employee during any day of a week during 20 weeks in a calendar year, regardless of whether the weeks were consecutive. The list of state unemployment insurance tax agencies, which will provide information for your specific state, can be found on the Department of Labor Web site, http://workforcesecurity.doleta.gov/unemploy/agencies.asp .

Federal Requirements for Family or Medical Leave

While it probably will not apply to solo or small firm practices, it is worth mentioning the Family and Medical Leave Act (FMLA). The FMLA only applies to employers with 50 or more employees for each working day during each of 20 or more workweeks during a calendar year. Very generally speaking, the FMLA requires employers to provide employees up to a total of 12 workweeks of unpaid leave during any 12-month period for the birth or care of a newborn child; the placement with the employee of a child for adoption or foster care; the care of an immediate family member with a serious health condition; or to take medical leave when the employee is unable to work because of a serious health condition.

The FMLA also has a provision that makes it unlawful to interfere with, restrain, or deny the exercise of FMLA benefits. It is also against the law to discriminate or retaliate against someone because of involvement in any proceeding related to the FMLA. The law is very broad and has been widely applied. An employee may bring claims to the Department of Labor, or may bring a private civil action for damages against an employer for violations of the act.

Polygraphs Generally Prohibited

Another federal law that only in rare occasions would apply to a solo or small firm practice is the Employee Polygraph Protection Act of 1988 (EPPA). The EPPA prevents employers from using lie detector tests, with certain very limited exceptions. The penalties for violation include civil money penalties from the Department of Labor of up to $10,000 per violation, and employment, reinstatement, promotion, and payment of lost wages and benefits for the employee.

Requirements for Accommodating Employees with Disabilities

The Americans with Disabilities Act requires employers with 15 or more employees to provide reasonable accommodations for known disabilities of a qualified applicant or employee. An employer is not required to make an accommodation that would impose undue hardship on the employer. Undue hardship is established by many factors, including cost of the accommodation in relation to the resources of the employer. However, undue hardship is determined on a case-by-case basis, and employers with greater resources are required to make a greater effort or expense than is required of an employer with fewer resources.

An employer does not have to reallocate essential job functions, but the employer must work with the employee to identify an accommodation that would not provide undue hardship, if possible.

Posting Requirements Regarding Employee Rights

All employers are required to post information regarding employee rights in the workplace. There are many companies that sell all-in-one posters for employers, but the posters are available from the Department of Labor and can be downloaded for free. The Web site with links to the posters of general applicability is found at http://www.dol.gov/elaws/asp/posters/posters.htm.

Wage and Hour Requirements

The wage and hour laws are the laws under which a solo or small firm practitioner is "most likely to be sued." The laws are not complicated, but are often misapplied by professional employers. The liability for violation of these laws is also very costly.

The Minimum Wage

The Fair Labor Standards Act (FLSA) sets the federal minimum wage. In May 2007, a federal minimum wage increase was signed by the President. The federal minimum wage will increase in three steps. The first step, which increased the federal minimum wage to $5.85 an hour, took effect on July 24, 2007. The second step increased the federal minimum wage to $6.55 on July 24, 2008. The third step increases the federal minimum wage to $7.25 on July 24, 2009.

Over half of the sates have minimum wage requirements higher than the current federal minimum wage rate. Therefore, it would be advisable to check your state's minimum wage requirements. A list of state minimum wage requirements can be found on the U.S. Department of Labor Web site at http://www.dol.gov/esa/minwage/america.htm.

The federal minimum wage requirements do not require an employer to provide vacation, sick, holiday, or severance pay, or holidays off, vacations, premium pay for weekend or holiday work, pay raises, or benefits. However, some states have more stringent requirements and you should review the state laws related to employee compensation and benefits for your state.

Overtime Compensation

With the exception of a few classes of exempt employees, employees who work over 40 hours a week are entitled to overtime compensation. Overtime compensation is one and one-half times an employee's hourly rate.

Employers are not required to pay an overtime rate unless the employee actually works more than 40 hours a week. If an employee earns an hourly wage for something other than work (i.e., a paid holiday, vacation day, or sick day), those non-working hours are included in the total hours worked.

On the other hand, private employers are not permitted to award comp time to employees in lieu of overtime. Employers often award comp time to employees in the form of an additional personal day. The only way an employer can use "comp time" is when the hours are both earned and used (i.e., cashed out) during the same pay period. In addition, the use of comp time cannot be a mandate from the employer; the employee must request the compensatory time off in lieu of the overtime pay.

For example, if you pay your employees every two weeks and the first week your receptionist works seven hours on Saturday, but the firm provides the receptionist 10.5 hours of paid time off during the second week of the pay period, the comp time would be permitted.

Another common misconception is that overtime is awarded by pay period, not by week. The workweek is not required to start on any specific day, but must remain consistent. If an employee works more than 40 hours during the workweek, the employee is entitled to overtime compensation even if the employee does not work more than 40 hours the second week of a two week pay period.

For example, many employers require that employees keep their time on a time sheet and that those time sheets are submitted every other week when it is time to process payroll. These time sheets often have a total for the first week, a total for the second week, and a combined total. If the total is simply the first and second week added, an employer could very easily miss its obligation to pay overtime compensation. If an employee works 42 hours the first week and 35 hours the second week, the employee is still due 2 hours of overtime compensation.

Salaried v. Hourly Employees

The biggest myth in wage and hour compensation is that employers do not have to pay salaried employees overtime, and simply providing a salary versus an hourly wage keeps an employer from having to pay overtime. This myth is *completely* untrue and provides the biggest exposure to liability.

Salaried employees are entitled to overtime compensation if they are not exempt from the overtime provisions. Do not assume that anyone is exempt. Unless you have read a provision in the Code of Federal Regulations or have read case law that specifically states a type of employee is exempt, you must assume your employees are not exempt and are entitled to overtime pay. Clerical workers, legal secretaries, filing clerks, and paralegals are not exempt employees.

Salaried employees can be paid overtime and that overtime is based on an hourly wage calculated using the employee's salary. Usually, a salaried employee is hired for a 40 hour work week. To determine the hourly rate, the salary is divided into 40 hours. The overtime rate is 1.5 times the calculated rate. Therefore, if an employer is paying $600 a week, the hourly rate would be $15 an hour and the overtime rate would be $22.50 an hour. If the employee routinely worked an extra hour or two per week or one Saturday a month, the exposure to the employer would be about $180 per month, or for three years of violation, $6,480. In addition, the employer might be required to pay liquidated damages and is required to pay attorney's fees and costs for the employee.

Employers usually try to be nice by providing a large salary for employees that sometimes work more than 40 hours a week, but end up facing very a great deal of liability. For example, if you pay an employee $800 per week because they routinely work 60 hours per week, the employee would be entitled to $30 per hour for all hours over 40 *on top of* the $800 already paid to the employee. In other words, the employee would be entitled to an additional $93,600 for three years of violation—just for back pay owed, not including penalties and attorneys' fees and costs.

The regulations provide for a written half-time agreement between the parties, which must clearly explain that the salary provided is to work more than 40 hours per week, but if the employee and employer agree to a half-time agreement, the employer still must pay the half-time for the hours over 40, and the half-time is determined by calculating the the number of hours worked in the week divided by the salary. In other words, the half-time amount would fluctuate week to week. Half-time agreements are too difficult to properly administer and are not advisable.

Exempt Employees

Exempt employees include bona fide executive, administrative, professional, outside sales, and certain computer employees. In order to be exempt, the employee must make a salary of at least $455 per week and the employee must meet the requirements found in the regulations. In an office setting, professionals often want to qualify their staff under the administrative exemption. However, one of the qualifications for the administrative exemption is that an administrative employee must exercise discretion and independent judgment and have the authority to make an independent choice free from immediate and direct supervision—in other words, whether the employee can deviate from established policies and procedures without approval.

A law office is unable to provide its staff with this type of authority. The rules regulating lawyers require that the lawyer take responsibility for the staff. Because of the nature of the business of a solo or small firm practice, it would be nearly impossible to qualify staff under the administrative exception for overtime.

The only person I can think of (other than an associate lawyer) who might qualify under one of the exemptions is an office manager. The executive exemption requires the employee to earn a minimum salary of $455 a week, the employee's primary duty must be managing the enterprise, the employee must direct the work of two or more employees, and the employee must have the authority to hire, fire, and advance employment of other employees.

However, the executive duties must be the primary duty of the exempt employee. In other words, the office manager cannot also be the managing partner's secretary. If the office manager is also a clerical worker, the employee is a "working supervisor" and is not exempt under from the overtime requirements.

Employers' Recordkeeping Responsibilities

The FLSA requires that employers keep records for non-exempt workers. The act requires that the following information be maintained:

1. Employee's full name and social security number.
2. Address, including zip code.
3. Birth date, if younger than 19.
4. Sex and occupation.
5. Time and day of week when employee's workweek begins.
6. Hours worked each day.
7. Total hours worked each workweek.
8. Basis on which employee's wages are paid (e.g., "$6 per hour," "$220 per week," "piecework")
9. Regular hourly pay rate.
10. Total daily or weekly straight-time earnings.
11. Total overtime earnings for the workweek.
12. All additions to or deductions from the employee's wages.
13. Total wages paid each pay period.
14. Date of payment and the pay period covered by the payment.

While the employer must keep track of the hours worked, the timekeeping method is not regulated and can be determined by the employer. The only requirement is that the method must be complete and accurate.

Employers are required to maintain the records for three years. The Division of Labor has the authority to request a review of these records, and it often does request to review the records when it receives a complaint by an employee or former employee.

While employers are only required to keep these records on non-exempt employees, employers often find themselves in a difficult situation when an employee has been misclassified as exempt and there are no records as required for non-exempt employees. In cases where salaried employees claim the employer failed to pay them overtime and they actually worked more than 40 hours per week, the burden is on the employer to prove that the employees did not work the 40 hours per week. As a result, employers should keep all of the information required by the Department of Labor for both exempt and non-exempt employees.

22 Good Reason, Bad Reason, No Reason in Particular: How to Fire an Employee

by Sheryl Sisk Schelin

You don't want to get a letter from me.

Don't get me wrong. I'm a fair correspondent; at times, even rather entertaining. But if you have employees in your law office, and you get a letter from *my* office, there's a pretty good chance that the letter inside will start off:

> Dear Fellow Attorney:
>
> I have been retained by your former employee, Rita Righteous, in conjunction with the events surrounding her termination of employment by you on . . .
>
> Please retain all correspondence, files, memoranda, etc. . . .
>
> If you are represented in this matter, please have your counsel contact me ....
>
> Sincerely,
> Sheryl Schelin
> Plaintiff's Attorney

Even if you've never practiced employment law, you are no doubt familiar with the concept of employment at will. Here's something to consider if this is the first time you've thought about the concept since studying for the bar exam: In almost every state in the United States, unless there's an employment contract in play, a worker can be fired (or can quit) for "a good reason, a bad reason, or no reason in particular" as the old saw goes. Of course, all generalizations, including the explanation in the preceding sentence, are false; the limitations on the employment at will doctrine truly threaten to swallow the whole (if they haven't already digested the meal in some states and moved on to dessert by now).

This chapter is all about how to avoid getting one of those letters from me, or a similar one from another attorney who practices plaintiff's employment law; it explores the concept and the practicalities of firing staff from the perspective of that old saying, starting with "good reasons"—the termination of an employee for cause.

Good Reasons

What offense warrants firing in your book? If you're an employer, you need to know that from the outset and to communicate that sufficiently to your employees.

Most of us can agree on one simple premise: terminating employees is neither easy nor desirable. Given our 'druthers, we'd all prefer working with employees to improve their performance over firing them. The reason is simple: firing employees opens a Pandora's box of horrors. High emotion, copious amounts of drama, decimated employee morale, even lawsuits—all these and more are the "parting gifts" for the unfortunate employer who draws the short straw in the termination sweepstakes.

Unfortunately, it *is* sometimes necessary. As long as humans are capable of imperfection, one bad apple can really do a number on the work product for the whole bunch. Therefore, take a moment to determine what those fireable offenses are. Then, take the time to communicate those reasons to your staff in reasonably plain language. Make them part of your personnel policy manual—you *do* have one of those, right?

The Counseling Approach

Because even the best workers have bad days that sometimes develop into weeks of slipping performance—and because sometimes new hires struggle with tasks and responsibilities—you should be prepared to implement the counseling approach for workers with identifiable performance issues.

- **Identify the issue.** The nature of the problem will determine whether a corrective plan is warranted or appropriate, and the steps such a plan should include.
- **If appropriate, develop a plan of correction.** Outline the specific steps the employee would have to take to win back your trust and approval.
- **Counsel the employee, and document the incident.** A private, after-hours meeting with the employee, conducted in a manner that's professional, yet "light" in tone, is crucial. Even more crucial: putting it all in writing and placing that document in the employee's personnel file.
- **Secure the employee's written acknowledgment.** An employee's signature on a document setting forth the issue and the plan of corrective measures goes a long way towards disproving allegations of arbitrary behavior.
- **Document the results.** You must continue to observe the employee's performance and document both the measures taken and the results of those measures.
- **If satisfactory improvement is not made within a reasonable time, terminate.** What constitutes a reasonable time will, of course, depend on the offense, but in most cases a month is appropriate: long enough to allow for meaningful change, but not so long that the firm will suffer permanent damage if the worker fails to improve.

Bad Reasons

Contrary to the old saying, of course, there *is* such a thing as an impermissible "bad reason" to fire an at-will employee. These prohibitions are found both in statutory schemes (federal and state) and in the common law of your jurisdiction. A complete discussion of these prohibitions is well beyond the scope of this chapter, but a brief discussion is in order.

Alphabet Soup: FMLA, ADA, ADEA, and . . . er . . . Title VII

At the federal level, a host of acronyms prevent discriminatory firings on the basis of protected class membership or characteristics. These "bad reasons" include:

- age (workers over 40 are protected by the Age Discrimination in Employment Act);
- disability (Americans With Disabilities Act, and some employers are covered by the Rehabilitation Act as well);
- race, color, religion, sex, and national origin (Title VII).

In addition, employers are prohibited from firing workers as a form of retaliation for exercising their rights under any of these laws, including the Family and Medical Leave Act. State laws, of course, vary widely but may echo or expand upon these protections, so you must take the time to become familiar with your duties in this regard.

At both the federal and state levels, government agencies charged with enforcement of the respective laws have websites that may offer all the preventative guidance you need. The Equal Employment Opportunity Commission, for example, has a Web site that provides the full texts of the laws it enforces, as well as guidance materials and FAQs (frequently asked questions and answers thereto) that help employers in this regard.

Common Law Protections: Handbooks as Contracts and "Public Policy"

Two other general sources of restrictions on the previously unfettered right to fire at will are the so-called handbook cases and the concept of wrongful termination in violation of public policy.

In handbook cases, plaintiffs argue that, notwithstanding the employment at will status they otherwise might have enjoyed, the employer's personnel manual or handbook created a contract between the two parties that governed the employment relationship. In the context of termination, these cases frequently focus on whether the disciplinary provisions were specific enough and couched in mandatory language that would have created a contractual right and corresponding duty on the part of the employer to discipline employees *only* in line with those provisions. Check your state statutes, however, as there may be a safe harbor provision that allows for prominent disclaimers to head off this claim and protect the employer from liability under this theory.

Termination as a violation of public policy was a judicial construct that developed to prevent employers from doing nasty things like firing workers for heeding jury duty summonses. Typically limited to fairly egregious behavior such as that, the specific scope of this doctrine, if it exists in your state, will be delineated by the factually-specific case law in your jurisdiction.

Avoiding Allegations of "Bad Reasons"

The bad news first: you can't entirely prevent an allegation that you fired a worker by engaging in discrimination. Even the most open-minded, liberally inclined employers can find themselves on the wrong end of a discrimination charge. It's simply human nature: if we're a member of a class that's been so commonly discriminated against that a legislative fix was enacted, we tend to see the shadow of that ghost when bad things happen to us and we don't have any other acceptable explanation as to *why*. We all want to believe the best about ourselves. Sometimes that means thinking the worst of others.

But you can take certain actions now to lessen the impact of such charges, and make it much less likely that they'll "stick" in any future legal proceeding.

- **Take the issue seriously**. Draft a policy prohibiting discrimination on the basis of any protected class or characteristic and include it in your handbook or manual.
- **Offer training on the policy**. Make sure everyone understands how to report a claim of discrimination, and make it easy for employees to do so. Note: it's best to use third party providers for this training, as tempting as it might be to do it yourself. And make sure *all attorneys* attend, as well as your support staff; it's

important for your employees to see you subject yourself to the same expectations you hold for them.

- **Enforce the policy evenly and consistently.** Don't allow what you perceive to be a harmless joke to fly without comment. There may well be no ill intent on the part of the individual telling the joke, but all it takes to sway a jury's sentiment out of your favor is one later-terminated plaintiff testifying that you, the boss/defendant, never reprimanded the individual. And as you are probably already all too aware, we simply cannot count on juries sharing our senses of humor or our sensitivities (or lack thereof).
- **Document *all* performance issues**. Without a doubt, this is the number one reason why the recently terminated seek my services in the first place. They tell a story of consistently good reviews, perhaps marred by some interpersonal conflicts and a few inappropriate (if questionably so) jokes, punctuated rudely by a termination without any explanation. When I ask, "Did you ever receive counseling or a write-up on any performance issue, even just a comment made in passing?" the answer is almost always "Never." Yet, the employer may well have a valid reason for the termination. You'd just never know it to look at the file. Bottom line: You must overcome your aversion to putting "bad stuff" in writing, and keep that file accurate and up to date.

No Reason In Particular

And what about the genuine case of "no reason in particular"? You can't really articulate anything the worker does or doesn't do, that would constitute an egregiously fire-able offense. But neither does the employee add anything to your team. There's nothing to correct, *per se*, so counseling would be ineffective. Perhaps it's a true personality conflict, as overused as that phrase may be, or perhaps you just think you can do better.

Here, the fast and direct approach is best:

- "We're going in a different direction with this position."
- "I'm going to be restructuring the office organization."

- The ubiquitous and vague "It's just not working out."

In other words: the less said, the better. Offer a reference (and make it a good one, if you can do so honestly . . . better yet, have it ready to go when you break the news), and wish them well.

As a Practical Matter

While no two situations are identical, and thus what works for one might backfire in another, you can and should think about the mechanics of terminating the employee before actually calling the employee into your office for that little chat. Consider the following practical pointers:

- **Whenever possible, avoid terminating on a Friday.** The person you fire will have the entire weekend to stew and get angry (or angrier), without having any constructive outlet for the natural fear that comes with being terminated from employment. The result: the firing seems increasingly unjust to the ex-employee, whose first call on Monday morning might well be to an employment lawyer, instead of the local Employment Commission. *Exception*: if it's a matter of personal safety, illegal actions (such as theft or violence), or some other serious malfeasance, don't wait—fire as soon as possible, and if that happens to be Friday at the close of business, so be it.
- **Whenever possible, terminate after the rest of the staff have left for the day, or well before they arrive**. Your soon-to-be-ex-employee will appreciate not having to run the gauntlet of well-meaning or merely curious coworkers.
- **Keep the tone serious and professional.** Don't make jokes in an attempt to inject a little levity or lighten the atmosphere. Firing is unpleasant. It's supposed to be. And nothing you say or do is going to make it enjoyable for the person who's being fired. Respect his or her feelings and do them the courtesy of allowing them to feel bad.
- **Under no circumstances give in to your own emotion.** I've heard of it all, I'm pretty sure: bosses who raged and ranted, bosses who threw things—even bosses who cried while they

were terminating workers. The only possible outcome of such high emotion will be to call even more attention to your role in the event, and further prompt the ex-employee to seek legal counsel. Whatever you do, remain in control. If you can't, get someone else to do it.

- ***Never* fire a worker in any way other than in person and face to face.** This might be the age of voice mail and text messaging, but these are sure-fire ways to enrage your former worker and get public sympathy on his or her side, to boot. Do your firing face to face—"live and in person"—and if that means having to wait a few days, then wait.
- **Skip the waivers and releases**. It's questionable whether any waiver signed in the immediate wake of a termination from employment would be deemed valid in any event, and after the employee gets home and thinks about it some more, he or she is sure to have some questions about your choice to seek the release in the first place. If there are legal issues which must be resolved, then it is highly advisable to do so only through legal counsel, allowing the employee time to seek their own counsel, in order to avoid claims of overreaching or intimidation.
- **Offer severance pay and a good reference, if you can**. If you're in a position to do so, and it's warranted, severance pay can go a long way towards heading off disgruntlement. And yes: this, you *can* condition on the employee's execution of a waiver or release of all claims against you. Likewise, have a generic "To Whom It May Concern" reference letter typed up, signed, and ready to hand to the employee on the spot. **Allow the worker sufficient time to clean out the work area, and double-check that they have everything.** Don't rush the worker out the door, and while you want to ensure nothing is improperly taken from the office (files, supplies, equipment, etc.), neither do you want to be too obvious about it. This is a good job for a mid-level worker, or another lawyer. If you can possibly manage it, though, avoid playing security guard yourself.
- **Clean up what's left**. Changing locks if necessary, changing passwords, administrative and bookkeeping paperwork, dealing with questions of remaining staff members — this is the aftermath of the termination process, but it's no less important.

Don't delay in managing matters related to technological and physical security; whatever needs to be done should be done immediately, if at all possible.

As for staff, their questions and concerns are understandable, but you should be cautious in revealing too much. For one thing, both your business and the former worker have some privacy interests at stake. Avoiding the issue entirely, however, is not advisable, as it will merely create an atmosphere of mistrust and rampant rumor-mongering. Confront it head on, as much as you can, and offer reassurance to those who remain by declining to tell tales.

Conclusion

Will terminating an employee ever be one of your favorite parts of the job? Clearly not—and if it is, you have bigger problems than managing your staff. But with a bit of careful planning, some empathy, and a dose of foresight, you can manage to get through the unpleasantness relatively unscathed. Perhaps your office can even emerge a bit stronger as a team, with increased confidence in you as the team captain for having managed the termination so skillfully.

Termination Checklist

Follow these steps for a smooth-as-possible termination meeting:

I. Announce the purpose of the meeting. Discuss the reasons in general. There is no need to go into specifics or recount all your documentation.
II. Let the employee know that the decision is final. If you have any sort of grievance procedure, let the employee know what the steps are to take advantage of it. It's most helpful to have this in written form.
III. Tell the employee that the decision was a consensual one among management, if applicable.
IV. Give the employee the effective date of termination and the exit interview form. Stress that the questionnaire is optional but would be helpful to address any concerns the employee would like to point out.
V. Have a written explanation of any benefits you're prepared to offer (severance, insurance, accrued vacation or sick pay compensation, re-employment assistance, etc.).
VI. Present the final paycheck, or have the employee confirm the address for the final check to be mailed to the employee.
VII. Collect all passwords from the employee; confirm the password before the employee leaves.
VIII. Take possession of all office keys, file cabinet keys, car keys, credit cards, and other office property.
IX. If applicable, give the employee the form reference letter.
X. Allow the employee sufficient time to clean out his or her desk and say his or her goodbyes, assuming the employee is in control (even if sad or angry).
XI. After the employee leaves, let other employees know of the termination (without specifics being offered, of course) and arrange for pick-up of work tasks, if necessary, pending a new hire.

Exit Interview Questionnaire

Name: ____

Date: ____________________

Position: ____

Dates of employment: ____________________

Reason for departure from firm: ___________________________

____

On a scale from 1 (abysmal, couldn't be worse) to 10 (superlative, couldn't be better), please rate your experience at our firm with the following criteria in mind:

Relationship with coworkers	1	2	3	4	5	6	7	8	9	10
Relationship with immediate supervisor(s)	1	2	3	4	5	6	7	8	9	10
Relationship with attorneys	1	2	3	4	5	6	7	8	9	10
Relationship with clients	1	2	3	4	5	6	7	8	9	10
Firm's employment policies and practices	1	2	3	4	5	6	7	8	9	10
Firm's work procedures and routines	1	2	3	4	5	6	7	8	9	10
Training	1	2	3	4	5	6	7	8	9	10
Opportunities for growth and	1	2	3	4	5	6	7	8	9	10

What can the firm do more effectively or, perhaps, for the first time to improve the working conditions, lead to a more efficient office, or create an atmosphere more conducive to job satisfaction?

____

____

____

____

Is there any practice or policy that you believe to be especially helpful and therefore should be continued or increased?

____

____

____

____

Is there anything else you think we should be made aware of, or that you want us to know?

____

____

____

____

____

____

Signed: ____________________________ Date: ____________________

A Form Reference Letter

May 2, 2009

To Whom It May Concern:

I understand that you have requested a reference for Anne Smith as a paralegal for
potential employment.

It is the policy of this firm to respond to requests for references with the following
information only:

- Confirmation of employment
- Position
- Salary
- Dates of Employment

Mrs. Smith worked for this office as a paralegal from October 2, 2006 through
September 18, 2008, with her final salary being $29,500.

If I may be of any additional assistance, please feel free to contact me.

Regards,

Amy Attorney, Esq.

A Form "To Whom It May Concern" reference letter typed up, signed, and ready to hand to the discharged employee on the spot

May 1, 2009

To Whom It May Concern:

I recommend Anne Smith as a paralegal for employment.

Ms. Smith was an employee of my office, Jones Law Offices, for two years, between 2006 and 2008. During that time, she performed several key office functions, namely:

- Calendaring all court deadlines and hearings
- Setting up and organizing case files
- Pre-interviewing witnesses for personal injury litigation
- Preparing draft documents for attorney review

Ms. Smith is eligible for rehire.

Regards,

Amy Attorney, Esq.

If you do get a letter from me—or some other plaintiff's employment lawyer—follow these steps:

- Notify your insurer, if applicable.
- Segregate the employee's file form others, and go through the file for completeness. Make a note of anything that should be in the file but isn't, and attempt to locate missing documents. Make note of your efforts.
- Collect any and all e-mails that might be remaining on your hard drives, either from, to, or about the employee in question. Take steps to prevent spoliation of all documentary evidence, including these e-mails.
- Make a preliminary investigation into the claims in the letter, if any. Talk to employees and other lawyers individually. If at all possible, have these interviews as close to each other as possible to minimize conversations that might taint or affect the information received.
- If harassment or discrimination is an issue, gather your resources establishing that you have a policy prohibiting the discrimination, a mechanism in place to receive and investigate complaints, and records to show whether a complaint was made and what the outcome of the resulting investigation was. This will assist you in meeting the *Faragher/Ellerth* affirmative defense burden.
- Consult with an employment defense specialist. Ask the lawyer to review your file and the initial letter, and to give an opinion about the allegations and any possible defenses.
- Discuss with partners, if applicable, or decide for yourself whether you want to make an offer and on what terms the offer should be made.

Afterword

We'd like to claim that this is the only resource a solo or small firm lawyer will ever need about staff in the law office, but we can't. State and federal laws change faster than the shelf life of this book.

Lawyers in solo and small firm practice should familiarize themselves with:

- Employer's Tax Guide, Publication 15, Circular E, published by the Internal Revenue Service (http://www.irs.gov/publications/p15/index.html). This guide is a goldmine of information about income tax withholding, FICA, and FUTA (federal unemployment deposits), record keeping, fringe benefits, making tax deposits, definitions of an employee, obtaining that Employer Identification Number (EIN), and even more.
- Employment Eligibility Verification. Employers must verify that every new employee is legally eligible to work in the United States by completing the U.S. Citizenship and Immigration Services (USCIS) Form I-9 (http://www.uscis.gov).
- New Hire Reporting. Employers must report any new employee, as well as any terminated employee, to the state child support agency. The protocol is explained at the Federal Office of Child Support Enforcement (http://www.acf.hhs.gov/programs/cse/newhire/employer/private/).
- State tax codes.

Index

E

P

V

W